FOOD LOVER'S
GUIDE TO
HONOLULU

JOAN NAMKOONG

3565 Harding Avenue
Honolulu, Hawai'i 96816
phone: (808) 734-7159
fax: (808) 732-3627
e-mail: sales@besspress.com
http://www.besspress.com

Design: Carol Colbath

Photo on page 50 by Douglas Peebles

Photographs may not represent actual items served or sold at
restaurants and shops included in the book.

Library of Congress Cataloging-in-Publication Data

Namkoong, Joan.
  Food lover's guide to Honolulu /
Joan Namkoong.
      p.   cm.
  Includes illustrations, glossary,
index.
  ISBN 1-57306-258-8
  1. Restaurants - Hawaii - Honolulu -
Guidebooks. 2. Farmers' markets -
Hawaii - Honolulu - Guidebooks.
3. Grocery trade - Hawaii - Honolulu -
Guidebooks. 4. Food - Guidebooks.
I. Title.
TX354.5.N36 2006   381.4-dc21

Printed in China

CONTENTS

INTRODUCTION

Having grown up in Hawai'i and having traveled to many parts of the world, I know that there's no better place to eat than in Hawai'i. When it comes to food, this is a food lover's paradise. There's Hawaiian food, the Polynesian-based menu that everyone who lives here embraces. There are ethnic foods that span the globe, offering different tastes for adventurous palates. And there's local food, the mingling of ethnic cuisines that has created unique dishes we call our own.

This guide will take you on a food lover's tour of Honolulu—from Hawai'i Kai to Kalihi—to experience the best this city has to offer: food stores, farmers' markets, unique dishes and food products, festivals and, of course, restaurants, cafes and hole-in-the-wall eateries that make up the vibrant food scene in Honolulu.

Included in this volume is a carefully selected list of locally owned businesses that perpetuate the food traditions of the islands and utilize the products of Hawai'i in their menus. These are the places where I seek out good food— places I think are some of the best for food in Honolulu. And I've included some recipes, too, for classic Hawai'i dishes.

The information presented is as current as possible at press time. Locales, hours of operation and even menus change; to verify information, call before visiting the numerous places listed.

Here's to good eating in Honolulu!

HAWAI'I'S FOOD EVOLUTION

Food defines life and culture in Hawai'i: it is the focal point of conversations, gatherings, celebrations and everyday life in the islands. After all, it was a food product—sugar—that formed the diverse melting pot of people and culture that defines Hawai'i today.

The first Polynesians to arrive in the islands brought with them a meager supply of food that included pigs, chickens, dogs, sweet potatoes and, of course, taro, the staple of the Hawaiian diet. Taro, its corm cooked and pounded into a starchy paste called poi, and its leaves and stems eaten as vegetables, was not only sustenance for the people but a symbol of the 'ohana and social order of Hawaiian culture.

When Captain Cook arrived in the Hawaiian Islands in 1778, the native Hawaiian diet began to change as cows, horses, sheep, goats and a variety of fruits and vegetables were introduced. Salt beef and salt salmon became protein staples; hardtack biscuits, a staple of sailing vessels, were introduced, and Christian missionaries from New England added to the food supplies of the islands.

In the last half of the 19th century, the growth of the sugar industry fueled the fires of immigration from other parts of the world. From Southern China came the first wave of sugar plantation workers, bringing with them today's starch staple, rice. The Japanese followed, and then the Koreans, Filipinos, Puerto Ricans and Portuguese. Soy sauce, ginger, garlic, chili peppers, bread, beans and a multitude of other foods became part of the islands' pantry. The sharing of ethnic foods by workers in the field at lunchtime or by home cooks over the backyard fence began to define Hawai'i's food culture, blending and adapting ingredients and flavors into what we call local food, the unique dishes and flavors that are evident in Hawai'i's cuisine today.

In the first half of the 20th century, American foods and dietary standards became more prominent in the diets of islanders as school lunch programs were established and canned and frozen food products made their way across the Pacific to Hawai'i.

Sugar and pineapple were the primary agricultural products and industry in Hawai'i through the mid–20th century. Tourism began its growth, too, and with the advent of air transportation, Hawai'i became the dream holiday destination for millions of people. Talented chefs, mostly European trained, came to Hawai'i to head up the kitchens of the growing numbers of restaurants and hotels built to service the tourist trade. By the 1980s these chefs had established Continental cuisine as fine-dining fare in hotels and restaurants.

In 1988 Roy's Restaurant opened in the East Honolulu neighborhood of Hawai'i Kai, with entrepreneur and chef Roy Yamaguchi creating a new kind of East-West fusion on the dining plate. This was the start of a new breed of younger chefs, trained in Europe and America, who began to redefine Hawai'i's palates and menus.

Capitalizing on the concept of fresh, locally grown products and creative menus, a dozen chefs in Hawai'i, representing prominent hotels and their own restaurants, formed a loosely knit group known as the Hawai'i Regional Cuisine chefs. Their mission was to involve farmers and food producers in the planning and execution of their menus. Forming alliances with key growers and suppliers, the chefs began to insist on fresh produce from the land and ocean and supported those who provided them. The chefs began to change Continental menus to reflect the ethnic flavors and dishes found in island kitchens.

With their technical expertise, an abundant and growing pantry of ingredients and the increasing sophistication of resident and visitor palates, Hawai'i Regional Cuisine chefs succeeded in their mission of showcasing island food products and flavors and placing Hawai'i on the culinary map. Today, chefs throughout the islands have reinvented Hawai'i's cuisine, relying more on locally grown and produced food products and adding their creative flair and talent to "local food."

Food is a reflection of who we are in Hawai'i, a melting pot of ethnic groups whose diversity is shared at the table. The prominence of traditional foods during special celebrations, the elevated quality of everyday fare at humble eateries and the finesse of fine-dining restaurants all speak to the importance and ongoing evolution of Hawai'i's culinary tradition that draws on a multitude of international food cultures. Hawai'i is truly a unique place in the world of food.

LOCAL FOOD

Local food is Hawai'i's everyday food. It is a distinctive blend of flavors and combination of ingredients that has evolved over the years from the cooking of the various ethnic groups that have settled here. Local food is not fancy, nor is it served in fine-dining restaurants, though it could be imitated there. It is simply down-home comfort food found in countless markets and hole-in-the-wall establishments throughout Honolulu. "Local grindz," as it is sometimes called, is food worthy of exploration and food that you will come to love.

Some distinctions among local food will become apparent as you explore the many facets of island cuisine. First, rice is a staple of the island table. While poi is a Hawaiian staple and well loved by local folks, everyone eats rice. It's the white, sticky kind we like best and we like lots of it.

Shoyu is the universal condiment and seasoning in local food. Add a little to scrambled eggs, use it to season just about everything; *shoyu* is ubiquitous. We also thrive on teriyaki sauce, a combination of soy sauce, sugar, ginger and maybe a little sake. We love marinades of soy sauce with garlic, ginger, sesame, green onions and perhaps a little chili pepper. Instead of salt, we use shoyu, adding savoriness to our food as well.

Chili pepper water is another condiment you might see in local restaurants. It's a fiery mix of chili peppers, preferably small Hawaiian chili peppers, vinegar, salt and water. It's sprinkled on everything; Tabasco is a good substitution and is often seen on many tables.

Local food is boldly flavored and spicy, with an Asian bent. We like foods that are salty, though we have a sweet palate, too, one that seems to be getting sweeter with time. We like gravies and sauces, especially with rice. In terms of texture, we like foods light, soft and squishy, especially when it comes to breads and other baked goods.

We also love mayonnaise in Hawai'i, and Best Foods reigns (it's called Hellmann's east of the Mississippi). There's nothing better than a good local-style macaroni salad, in which the quantity of mayonnaise is crucial. Mayonnaise is often used when cooking fish to keep it moist and succulent. Tasty walnut shrimp in a Chinese restaurant relies on the creamy texture of mayo. Mayonnaise is even dressed up and served with breads at a restaurant as an alternative to butter. (Hoku's serves a dynamite *'ahi* spread; Alan Wong's serves a chili *aioli*). Yes, it makes for high-calorie eating, but hey, it's *'ono* (delicious)!

BREAKFAST FARE

Several combinations come to mind when we think about a local breakfast. Portuguese sausage, eggs and rice are a classic combination, served up even at McDonald's. Garlicky, spicy pork sausage, fried crisp, accompanied by eggs, your style, and steamed

white sticky rice. Spam, vienna sausage, ham, bacon and fried fish are alternatives to the Portuguese sausage loved by local folks. Substitute the white rice with fried rice (see Rice, below) for another classic combination.

Perhaps more unique is the *loco moco*: a fried beef patty (ground beef mixed with onions, breadcrumbs and seasonings) with steamed white sticky rice, eggs your style, all smothered in brown gravy. It's a dish that originated at Cafe 100 in Hilo, Hawai'i, and persists today in many forms in many locales.

RICE

Rice isn't unique to Hawai'i, but it's an important part of what we eat. Besides poi, the Hawaiian starch staple made from pounded taro, rice is Hawai'i's other starch staple. Everyone here eats rice, in good quantity, and it's the sticky kind we love. Calrose is the standard rice, medium-grain and sticky, cooked in a rice cooker at home and at local eateries. Premium rices, sometimes called sushi rice, are also gaining in popularity. They tend to be shorter-grain varieties that originated in Japan, where rice is prized, and they, too, are sticky. We don't like long, loose grains as well and we really don't like Uncle Ben's.

Leftover rice is never thrown away. Refrigerated overnight (or frozen), leftover rice is used to make fried rice. This Chinese invention has been modified in Hawai'i to become a meal in itself, the best of which consists of rice, bacon, luncheon meat (usually Spam), *kamaboko*, *char siu*, egg, green onion and seasonings like soy or oyster sauce. Kim chee or *lup cheong* can be tossed in, too. Fried rice and egg for breakfast is a winning combination.

The Portuguese contributed Portuguese sweet bread to the local diet, an egg-and-butter-rich sweet dough baked to golden yellow perfection. Eat it toasted with butter and guava jam, make it into French toast or bread pudding—it's delicious!

THE PLATE LUNCH

The plate lunch is the epitome of what we call local food. This is comfort food, simple down-home cooking, traditionally eaten at lunchtime, served up on paper plates or, today, in Styrofoam containers, and a reflection of Hawai'i's ethnic melting pot.

The traditional plate lunch starts with "two scoops rice," sticky and white, taken from Asian cuisine. Then there's "salad," which means macaroni salad, mayonnaise-laden, with bits of tuna, cabbage and carrots, displaying the influences of American home economists, institutional food, school lunches and military mess halls. The entrée, or protein, can be from any culture—Hawaiian *kālua* pork, Japanese teriyaki beef or chicken, Korean *kal bi*, Filipino adobo, fried fish, crisp *panko*-coated chicken or pork known as *katsu*, Chinese oyster sauce chicken, meat loaf or spaghetti. It is served as a *haole* portion, meaning large. Pickled radish or kim chee, from Asian cuisine, may be the only vegetable on the plate; plate lunches are about protein and starch. As you can imagine, a plate lunch is filling and more than enough food and calories for a day.

You'll find plate lunches served up at small cafes, diners and lunch wagons wherever you go in Hawai'i. You could say they are our hole-in-the-wall restaurants. They are economical: a typical plate lunch costs about $5 to $8, depending on the entrée. By the way, sometimes the mayonnaise-laden macaroni salad can be substituted with a tossed green salad, making a plate lunch just a little healthier. And some places offer brown rice instead of white.

HAWAI'I'S MACARONI SALAD

Macaroni salad made in Hawai'i has a unique flavor and texture, the result of the combination of ingredients and the generous helping of Best Foods mayonnaise. You can't skimp on the mayonnaise. Besides, the creaminess of this salad perfectly balances the salty flavors of teriyaki or *kal bi* or other local foods.

1 tablespoon salt
1 pound elbow macaroni
1 can tuna, drained
1 cup finely shredded carrot
1 cup finely shredded cabbage
1/4 cup grated sweet onion
3 hard-cooked eggs, coarsely grated
2 teaspoons salt
2 teaspoons finely ground white pepper
4 to 5 cups mayonnaise

In large pot, bring 8 quarts of water to a boil. Add 1 table-spoon of salt and macaroni and cook until tender. Drain, rinse with cool water and drain again.

While macaroni is warm, mix with remaining ingredients, using about 3 cups of mayonnaise. Cover and refrigerate. When salad is chilled, add additional mayonnaise. Keep chilled until ready to serve. Serves 10 to 12.

Ethnic plate lunches may be a little healthier: Korean, Chinese and Filipino plates have more protein-vegetable combinations among their selections. Some places offer miniplates that make a lot of sense if you have a small appetite or are counting calories or fat grams.

Exploring local food is easy to do: countless places serve up a roster of local favorites. The places listed here have been around for a long time, doing what they do best, and will hopefully be around for some time to come so we can satisfy our local food cravings.

WHERE TO GO FOR BREAKFAST AND PLATE LUNCHES

Diamond Head Market and Grill

3575 Campbell Ave.
732-0077
Market open daily 7:30 a.m.-9 p.m.; deli closes at 8:30 p.m.
Grill open daily 10:30 a.m.-8:50 p.m.
Parking available

Plate lunches here are not your standard local fare. Expect grilled *'ahi* steaks, *char siu* chicken, shrimp with garlic butter, grilled salmon and more, devised by chef/owner Kelvin Ro, who embellishes with wasabi butter sauces, balsamic butter glazes, port wine reductions and sauces you'd expect to find in a fine-dining venue. But you'll also find comforting favorites like his Hawaiian-style hamburgers (seasoned beef with onions and bread) topped with portobello mushrooms, *char siu* and *kal bi*. Next door to the takeout grill area is more tempting local-style food like sushi and *bentos*, breakfast pastries (blueberry cream cheese scones are very popular) and desserts, prepared salads, and entrées to take home to heat and eat. It's a one-stop spot for good food at affordable prices.

Fort St. Bar and Grill
745 Fort Street Mall
523-1500
Lunch Mon.-Fri. 10:30 a.m.-2 p.m.
Pupus Wed.-Fri. 4 p.m.-10 p.m.
Parking in Topa Tower; enter from Nimitz Hwy.

Chicken prepared a dozen different ways—*shoyu*, *mochiko*, spicy, chili orange, oyster sauce, mushroom, miso, teriyaki, hoisin, *liliko'i* barbecue, marinara and *katsu*—and favorites like beef stew and beef curry are served up to downtown business folks hankering for local comfort food. The requisite two scoops rice and salad (macaroni or green) accompany the generous portions. Head upstairs for a seat or sit in the park just outside before heading back to the workday. A popular spot for *pau hana* cocktails, too.

Golden Coin Bakeshop and Restaurant
1833 N. King St.
842-0866
Daily 5 a.m. to 8:30 p.m.
Parking available

1719 Liliha St.
528-2990
Daily 5:30 a.m. to 7:30 p.m.
Street parking

654 Ke'eaumoku St.
955-8386
Mon.-Thurs. 6 a.m.-10 p.m.; Fri. 6 a.m.-11 p.m.; Sat., Sun.
    7 a.m.-10 p.m.
Street parking

The name of this chain doesn't even hint at what it serves: Filipino plate lunches. For breakfast you can get house-made *arroz caldo* or *longanisa* sausage with eggs and rice. For lunch and dinner choose from among a long list of Filipino dishes like pork adobo, *dinuguan, pinakbet,* pork *guisantes, kare kare,* and *lechon,* served up with rice or *pancit.* Hot *pan de sal,* literally just out of the oven, is always available, as is an array of Filipino desserts, including *halo halo.* This company was started in the mid-1980s by a family from the Philippines. They also serve up *manapua;* in fact Golden Coin wholesales *manapua* to big-box retailers and fast-stop places. The company also has two restaurants in Waipahu.

Kaka'ako Kitchen

Ward Centre
1200 Ala Moana Blvd.
596-7488
Mon.-Thurs. 7 a.m.-9 p.m.; Fri., Sat. 7 a.m.-10 p.m.; Sun. 7 a.m.-
    6 p.m.
Parking available

For the best fried rice in Honolulu and a great *loco moco,* this Styrofoam-service sit-down/takeout spot is tops. It also has great pastries—morning buns, banana taro bread, pumpkin ginger bread—all pretty wonderful. Lunch and dinner plates feature all sorts of local favorites—five-spice *shoyu* chicken, crispy sweet chili chicken, beef stew, meat loaf, *'ahi* wraps—with a dose of green salad and brown rice if you want to eat a little healthier. This is an upscale local eatery in terms of food, reflecting the fine-cuisine attitude of its owner Russell Siu of 3660 on the Rise. You can even enjoy a glass of wine or a beer here.

L&L Drive-Inn

1711 Liliha St., the original
533-3210
Mon.-Fri.. 9 a.m.-9:30 p.m.; Sat. 8 a.m.-9 p.m.; Sun. 8 a.m.-
    4 p.m.
Street parking

Ala Moana Center
1450 Ala Moana Blvd.
942-8884
Mon.-Sat. 6:30 a.m.-9 p.m.; Sun 6:30 a.m.-7 p.m.
Parking available

Fifteen other locations in Honolulu
www.hawaiianbarbecue.com

L&L is one of the islands' favorite dining spots for local fare. Plates are large and prices are low, a combination that makes local folks quite happy. Chicken *katsu*—thin pieces of chicken, breaded and fried—is perhaps most renowned here. Eddie Flores and Johnson Kam opened the first L&L on Liliha St. in 1959 and now have 50-plus franchised locations plus L&L Hawaiian Barbecue on the U.S. mainland, where it is making major inroads. It is simply a local experience to eat at L&L.

Likelike Drive Inn Restaurant

745 Keʻeaumoku St.
941-2515
Daily, 24 hours a day
Parking available

Over a half-century ago, James and Alice Nako started Likelike, a local-style diner with a menu designed to please local palates.

Where else can you find canned soup, fried or deviled egg sandwiches and Jell-O with whipped cream alongside fried rice, *saimin*, *loco moco*, burgers, chili and rice and other local staples? What's interesting here is, you can get anything on the menu, any time of day. The Nakos are gone now, but their daughter and son-in-law, the Hayashis, and the next generation carry on the tradition of good local grindz.

Patti's Chinese Kitchen
Makai Market at Ala Moana Center
1450 Ala Moana Blvd.
946-5002
Mon.-Sat. 9 a.m.-9 p.m.; Sun. 10 a.m.-7 p.m.
Parking available

Back in 1967, Calvin Chun was probably the first to offer Chinese plate-lunches-to-go in a town that had a lot of small sit-down Chinese restaurants. Not only that, he introduced the concept of rice or noodles plus two, three or four dishes on a plate at set prices, an idea now used by a number of ethnic takeout places. Patti's survives today because of its freshly cooked Chinese food that has that "local taste" in the beef broccoli, pot roast pork, sweet-and-sour spareribs, lemon chicken and *char siu*. There are more than 20 items on the selection line, plus *manapua*, cookies, peanut candy and other local Chinese favorites, all made fresh daily on the premises. James and Patti Louie (she's the daughter and the restaurant's namesake) now run Patti's, which has been at Ala Moana Center since the beginning. Another location is at Pearlridge Center in 'Aiea.

Pu'uwainani's Plate Lunches

Parking lot at the corner of Halekauwila and South Streets
286-5388
Mon.- Fri. 10 a.m. to 1 p.m.
Street parking

"Gourmet-kine grinds" here are a bit more contemporary, like *'ahi* with sweet wasabi sauce, garlic mahimahi with stir-fry veggies, crab-stuffed salmon with white wine sauce. But stick to the traditional pork *guisantes*, hamburger steak, *misoyaki* butterfish and pork adobo and you can't go wrong. You can feel a little healthier by ordering brown rice or tossed salad, and miniplates are also a good idea.

Sam Choy's Breakfast, Lunch and Crab

580 N. Nimitz Hwy.
545-7979
www.samchoys.com
Breakfast Mon.-Fri. 6:30-10:30 a.m., Sat., Sun. 7-11 a.m.
Lunch Mon.- Thurs. 10:30 a.m.-3 p.m.; Fri. 10:30 a.m.-4 p.m.;
    Sat., Sun. 11:30 a.m.-4 p.m.
Dinner Mon.-Fri. 5-9:30 p.m.; Sat., Sun. 5-10 p.m.
Parking available

Celebrity chef Sam Choy loves his local food, and that's what this off-the-beaten-path restaurant is all about. Expect local favorites like fish and *kālua* pork *loco mocos*, beef stew, fried rice and eggs and our favorite Chinatown omelet with *lup cheong* and *char siu*. You can't go wrong with the *moemoe* (sleep sleep) *saimin* or the fried *poke* wrap, and there's a wide assortment of seafood and fish, all served up in bountiful portions. Enjoy it all with Sam's own Aloha Brews, made on the premises; the ambiance is casual, complete with fishing boat. You can get Sam Choy's more upscale local fare at his Diamond Head Restaurant, at 449 Kapahulu Ave.; 732-8645.

Side St. Inn
1225 Hopaka St.
591-0253
Mon.-Fri. 10:30 a.m.-1 p.m.
Bar open 2 p.m.-2 a.m. daily; kitchen serves food 4 p.m.-
     12:30 a.m.
Valet or street parking

By day, this is a terrific place for local-style plate lunches, just like its sister spot, Fort St. Bar and Grill. By night, Colin Nishida's place is a bar, a smoke-filled bar at that, with televisions blaring during sports events. But the pork chops, fried rice, *'ahi poke* and Nalo Greens salad are first-rate, so much so that Honolulu's celebrity chefs and their staffs hang out here during their off hours to eat, drink and relax. There's quite an extensive menu of good comfort food that's a bit salty—terrific with that cold beer, glass of wine (there's a wine list here) or other beverage.

Simply 'Ono
Kewalo Basin, Diamond Head end
Mon.-Sat. 10:30 a.m.-2 p.m.
255-2283
Metered parking lot

City Municipal Building
Mon.-Fri. 10:30 a.m.-2 p.m.
255-2283
City municipal parking lot

Lunch wagons are few and far between these days. But Cora Stevens and Harris Sukita, former big-name-hotel kitchen workers, run two of them, each with a decidedly different clientele and menu. At Kewalo Basin, they serve up local fare like hamburger steak, teriyaki chicken and baked spaghetti (quite delicious) to surfers, truck drivers, families at the beach and folks who work in the area. At the City Municipal Building location, plate lunches are more upscale, with fresh fish, rack of lamb, prime rib, pasta and roast turkey on the menu for city and state workers who like something different every day. At both locations you can get a green salad and garlic or brown rice instead of the usual macaroni salad and white rice. The owners prove that you can get good food for little money at Honolulu's lunch wagons.

Tsukenjo Lunch Wagon

Corner of Ward Ave. and Queen St.
Mon.-Fri. 10 a.m. to 2 p.m.
597-8151
Street parking

You'll recognize the orange-red truck parked at the corner of a furniture store by the line forming soon after it opens at midmorning. For more than 40 years, Tsukenjo has been serving up roast pork with gravy, turkey and dressing, meat loaf, corned beef hash, *chow fun*, fried chicken, hamburger steak and other local favorites with the requisite two scoops rice and salad. This is typical, tasty, good local fare and plenty of it for $6 or less. You can also visit Tsukenjo at 705 Cooke St., just a few blocks away.

KOREAN MARINADE FOR *PUL KO GI* OR *KAL BI*

This marinade is excellent for thin-sliced beef, beef short ribs or chicken, all of which should be cooked on a grill. For a terrific salad, add chili pepper flakes and dress torn romaine lettuce. Prepare this sauce, let the flavors blend for an hour, and then strain it and use it to season fresh *'ahi* for *poke*. This is a great sauce.

1 cup soy sauce
1/3 cup water
1 tablespoon minced garlic, about 3 to 4 cloves
2 teaspoons minced ginger
1/2 cup chopped green onions
2 tablespoons honey or brown sugar
2 tablespoons sesame oil
2 tablespoons toasted sesame seeds, ground

Combine all ingredients. Makes 1 1/2 cups. Store covered in refrigerator.

Yummy Korean Barbecue
Makai Market at Ala Moana Center
1450 Ala Moana Blvd.
946-9188
Mon.-Sat. 9 a.m.-9 p.m.; Sun. 9 a.m.-7 p.m.
Parking available

Koko Marina Shopping Center
7192 Kalaniana'ole Hwy.
395-4888

Mon.-Sat. 10:30 a.m.-8: 30 p.m.; Sun. 10:30 a.m.-8 p.m.
Parking available

Seven other locations in Honolulu

Peter Kim is the brains behind this string of Korean plate lunch
takeout eateries that offer more food than you can possibly eat, at
a reasonable price. Choose from entrées that include *kal bi*, *pul ko
gi*, chicken, spicy pork, meat *juhn* and several others. Then choose
four seasoned vegetable dishes, from kim chee, seasoned bean
sprouts, watercress, cabbage, potatoes, daikon and more. It will all
be served up with a heap of rice. Other Korean favorites are available too, like *mandoo*, *kook soo,* and tofu soup. This is strictly
Styrofoam takeout fare, though some locations offer limited seating. This chain of takeout eateries began in 1986; Tasty's BBQ and
Pearl's Korean BBQ are part of the same chain and serve essentially the same food. As is typical of local food eateries, there's quantity for sure, and quality here is also consistent.

Zippy's
Inside Sears at Ala Moana Center
1450 Ala Moana Blvd.
973-0870
Mon.-Sat. 6 a.m.-9 p.m.; Sun. 6 a.m.-7 p.m.
Parking available

4134 Wai'alae Ave.
733-3730
Daily, 24 hours a day
Parking available
Seven other locations in Honolulu
www.zippys.com

This local fast-food chain caters to the taste buds of islanders seeking value and comfort food. Its chili is renowned, served up with rice, sold by the bucket by school kids raising money for soccer teams and what have you. Plate lunches are standard two-scoop rice, salad and protein affairs; Zip packs are quite a deal. Napoleon Bakeries, known for their apple-filled puff pastry called Napples, are attached, offering pastries and desserts that cater to the sweet tooth of local folks. On a healthier note, Zippy's serves menus designed by local healthy-eating guru Dr. Terry Shintani. It also offers frozen foods to send to homesick local folks living on the mainland.

OKAZU YA

In Japanese, *okazu ya* is a shop specializing in side dishes. In Hawai'i, *okazu ya* means Japanese delicatessen, or deli. But these are obviously not New York–style delis, nor do they serve just Japanese side dishes. Delis provide a wide array of dishes from which you can make a Japanese plate lunch, though you may also encounter foods from other ethnic groups.

First choose your starch: sushi, *musubi, chow fun*, chow mein or all of the above. Then choose your side dishes: teriyaki beef, *shoyu* chicken, miso butterfish, tofu patties, *nishime*, *gobo*, fried fish, hot dogs, fried Spam, hash, tempura (sweet potato, vegetable or shrimp), fried chicken, *namasu* or other specialties. Don't forget the salad, mayonnaisey-rich macaroni or macaroni-potato salad that's really a vital part of the plate: a creamy, fatty foil to balance the soy sauce–based seasonings of the other dishes.

Delis are not known for serving a lot of vegetable dishes, though some may have a few stir-fries in their assortment. Delis serve down-home comfort foods, salty, sweet, tasty and great with

rice. It's best to get to a deli early: they open at 5 or 6 a.m. and are closed (because they are out of food) by 2 in the afternoon.

Traditional delis still wrap their plates in butcher paper and secure it with a rubber band. Styrofoam containers are more prevalent these days. Wooden disposable chopsticks are the proper eating implement. Rarely would you sit and eat at the *okazu ya*; this is takeout food, so head to the nearest beach or shady tree and enjoy.

Fukuya Delicatessen and Catering
2710 S. King St.
946-2073
Wed.-Sun. 6 a.m.-2 p.m.; closed Mon. and Tues.
Parking available; also street parking

Bright and welcoming, this family-run Mōʻiliʻili deli has been operating for close to 70 years, catering to generations of local folks who relish the simple home-style dishes prepared here. The selections are not extensive, but they are more than enough to fill a plate with favorites. *Musubi* with *shiso* and *furikake* are unique here; *maki sushi* is excellent here, as is the macaroni salad. Tofu patties, *teriyaki* beef and chicken and *misoyaki* butterfish are a must, as are *nishime* and *gobo*. *Mochi* and cookies are made here, too. Fukuya also offers catering. Patrons come and go quickly, so the limited number of parking spaces turn over in a matter of minutes.

Gulick Delicatessen

1512 Gulick Ave.
847-1461
Mon.-Sat. 5 a.m.-3 p.m.; Sun. 8 a.m.-2 p.m.
Street parking

Gulick Delicatessen has been in the Kalihi neighborhood for a quarter of a century and is one of Honolulu's best *okazu ya*. Amid stainless steel counters and glass display cases are more than 30 different items to choose from—Japanese, Chinese, Filipino, Hawaiian and American specialties that *kama'āina* savor. There are more than a dozen ways to have your rice (plain, sushi, *musubi*), at least ten different chicken preparations, and an assortment of beef, pork and fish dishes, plus noodles, salads, tempura and everything else you could possibly want to eat. It would take many visits to try everything here, and because it's made fresh daily, it's always *'ono*.

Construction workers are among the first customers, at 5 a.m., followed by office workers on their way downtown. During football season, this family-run deli adds items like *kal bi* and *poke* to its menu list for tailgating fans. And it will happily cater your next party with food everyone loves.

Finding street parking in this residential area is always difficult, but cruise the block and wait patiently for the next available
spot. It's worth the wait.

TERIYAKI SAUCE

There's nothing like the smell of teriyaki beef or chicken
on the grill, especially if you're at the beach. This salty-
sweet marinade and basting sauce will flavor your food and
give it that nice shiny glaze that teriyaki is all about.

1 cup soy sauce
1/2 cup mirin
1/2 cup sake
3/4 cup sugar
1 clove garlic, smashed
Quarter size piece of ginger, smashed

Combine all ingredients in a saucepan and bring to a boil.
Stir and lower heat to a simmer; simmer for 5 minutes.
Remove from heat and cool. Makes about 1 1/2 cups. Store
covered in refrigerator.

Nu'uanu Okazu Ya
1351 Nu'uanu Ave.
533-6169
Tues., Wed., Fri. Sat. 6 a.m.-2 p.m.
Street parking

For 28 years, the Nagamine family has been cooking up home-
style dishes that local folks love: teriyaki chicken and 'ahi,

nishime, gobo, macaroni salad, namasu and sushi. Everything here is quite tasty and delicious; be sure to try the fried rice *musubi*. We love the fact that they still wrap the paper plates in paper, secured with a rubber band. While there are a few tables, it's a take-away kind of place.

MANAPUA

Mea ʻono puaʻa, or Chinese pork cake, is also known as *manapua*. This delicious bun filled with *char siu* is also known as *char siu bao* in the lexicon of Chinese dim sum treats. Local-style *manapua* has lots of bright-red *char siu* in the center of a steamed white bun or a golden baked bun. The term *manapua* also refers to the genre of dumplings that includes half-moon, *pepeiao* and pork hash.

Manapua is unique to Hawaiʻi, quite different in size and taste from the *char siu bao* served up in dim sum restaurants in Honolulu. And food creativity has blossomed when it comes to

manapua. Newer versions of the steamed and baked buns are filled with *kālua* pork, spicy eggplant, sweet potato, and who knows what, depending on the maker. But the traditional steamed or baked pork cake still reigns as the best *manapua*.

Char Hung Sut

64 N. Pauahi St.

538-3335

Mon., Wed.-Sat. 5:30 a.m.-1:45 p.m.; Sun. 5:30 a.m.-12:45 p.m.; closed Tues.

Street parking; municipal lot within a block

Bat Moi Kam Mau opened this family business, known for its local-style *manapua*, pork hash, half-moon and *pepeiao*, in 1946. You can watch the preparations as you wait for your order, which is packed in a pastry box. Fillings are on the sweet side, catering to the local palate. This is strictly a food-to-go place with a limited menu, but local folks from throughout the state patronize this Chinatown institution.

Chun Wah Kam Noodle Factory

505 Kalihi St.

841-5303

Mon.-Fri. 6 a.m.-4 p.m.; Sat. 7 a.m.-4:30 p.m.; Sun. 7 a.m.-noon

Limited parking; try neighboring streets

This 50-plus-year-old noodle factory turns out a different array of *manapua*. Nelson Chun, the founder's son, has fun trying different fillings for his steamed buns: *kālua* pork, *shoyu*, honey-garlic, curry or barbecue chicken, teriyaki beef and others, in addition to the traditional *char siu, lup cheong* and black sugar. Choose from an assortment of Chinese specialties for a Chinese plate lunch, too.

Island Manapua Factory

811 Gulick Ave.
847-2677
Mon.-Sat. 5:30 a.m.-3 p.m.; Sun. 7 a.m.-1 p.m.
Parking available

Mānoa Marketplace
2752 Woodlawn Dr.
988-5441
Mon.-Fri. 7:30 a.m.-8 p.m.; Sat. 7:30 a.m.-7 p.m.; Sun. 8:30
    a.m.-5:30 p.m.
Parking available

The baked *manapua* here is one of the best because it has a nice proportion of tasty lean meat to bun. Pork hash is good here, too, capturing that local flavor with greasy undertones. This is a good spot for local Chinese food-to-go of all kinds. Crispy-skinned Chinese-style roast pork and lean *char siu* are excellent.

Kwong On

3620 A Wai'alae Ave.
734-4666
Mon.-Sat. 7 a.m.-3 p.m.
Street parking; municipal lot nearby

This Kaimukī outpost of local Chinese food has been here since 1966, with Chun Tsui Chin and William Chin keeping the *manapua* steaming. Traditional local favorites here are half-moons, pork hash, *pepeiao*, curry half-moon cakes, noodles, fried rice and stir-fry dishes. A convenient spot for East Honolulu residents craving some *chow fun*, roast chicken, spareribs, peanut candy and other Chinese treats.

Royal Kitchen
Chinese Cultural Plaza
524-4461
Mon.-Fri. 5:30 a.m.-4:30 p.m.; Sat. 6:30 a.m.-4:30 p.m.; Sun.
    6:30 a.m.-2:30 p.m.
Street parking

Best known for its baked *manapua*, Royal Kitchen is worth the walk to the edge of Chinatown. There's traditional *char siu* filling; Portuguese sausage, *kālua* pork, *lup cheong* , and curried chicken or vegetables are some of the other choices. For dessert try a bun filled with black sugar, coconut or Okinawan sweet potato. One bun is perfect for a snack, two for a delicious lunch. Pork hash, half-moons and other local Chinese favorites are made here too.

S A I M I N

Saimin is Hawai'i's favorite soup: Chinese egg noodles served in a steaming bowl of Japanese broth, topped with green onions, *char siu*, luncheon meat and fish cake. It's like chicken noodle soup, only much better. It is not Japanese *ramen*; it is *saimin* and unique to Hawai'i, found nowhere else in the world. It is served up at sporting events, movie theaters and, of course, in local food restaurants.

You'll find quick and easy versions at fast-food places and in the freezer section of the supermarket. But a properly made *saimin* boasts fresh noodles, crinkly and chewy, and a tasty broth based on Japanese *dashi*, usually a secret recipe of the proprietors of small shops that specialize in this local dish.

When you want to eat *saimin* like a local, you add a little soy sauce and a sprinkling of black pepper to your bowl of steaming noodles. With chopsticks in the right hand and *saimin* spoon in the left, you begin to eat, sipping broth with your spoon, lifting noodles out of the broth with your chopsticks and into your mouth or placing noodles into the spoon to eat. It's a ritual and a very delicious one at that.

Teriyaki beef on sticks is a natural accompaniment to *saimin*. *Won ton mein*, a combination of dumplings and noodles, is a popular variation, eaten with hot Chinese mustard and soy sauce. Here are some places that serve up *saimin*, made the old-fashioned way:

Boulevard Saimin
1425 Dillingham Blvd.
841-7233
Mon.-Sat. 9:30 a.m.-9 p.m.; Sun. 9:30 a.m.-4 p.m.
Parking available

Years ago, when McDonald's executives came to town, they were persuaded to add ethnic dishes to the menu. Boulevard Saimin is where they tried *saimin* and decided to add it to Hawai'i's repertoire of fast-food items sold under the golden arches.

Toshiaki Tanaka and his family started serving *saimin* in 1956, brewing up a broth of shrimp and seaweed that is a classic today. They also serve many variations on the *saimin* theme—topped with kim chee, teriyaki and Portuguese sausage. Plus there's a full array of local-style dishes like *loco moco*, chicken *katsu*, burgers, corned beef hash and more, all served up in this small 27-seat cafe.

Palace Saimin Stand

1256 N. King St.

841-9983

Tues.-Sat.; closed Sun and Mon.

Tues.-Sat. 11 a.m.-3 p.m.; Tues., Thurs.-Sat. 8-11:30 p.m.; closed Sun., Mon.

Limited parking; street parking

What sets this place apart from all the others is the broth, steaming hot, well flavored and classic. Setsuko Arakaki and her husband (he makes the broth) have been running this very small *saimin* stand for over 20 years. All you'll find on the menu are *saimin, won ton mein* and teriyaki beef sticks, but that's enough because that's why you're here.

Sekiya's Restaurant and Delicatessen

2746 Kaimukī Ave.
732-1656
Sun.-Thurs. 8:30 a.m.-10 p.m.; Fri., Sat. 8:30 a.m.-11 p.m.
Parking available

Sekiya's has been around since 1935, serving up steaming bowls of *saimin* and barbecued teriyaki beef sticks. The crinkly noodles are cooked al dente, retaining their chewiness, and they don't get mushy in the family's proprietary broth. The third generation of Sekiya's is now in the business, keeping the repertoire of *okazu ya* selections fresh each day and making sure the *oyako don* and tempura are perfect. And, of course, the *saimin*.

SPAM *MUSUBI*

Spam and other canned meats—Vienna sausage, Coral tuna, Libby's corned beef, Holmes sardines—are popular Hawai'i pantry items. They are convenient, they don't spoil in tropical heat, they are reasonably priced and, during World War II, they were available.

It's no secret: we do consume more Spam in Hawai'i per capita than anywhere else in the fifty states. It's a dubious distinction, but Spam and its many concoctions—Spam and eggs, Spam won tons, baked Spam topped with pineapple, the list goes on— are popular in Hawai'i. There is even a local snobbery attached to Spam: you have to eat Spam to be "local."

Salty Spam and rice are a perfect marriage. And what better way to eat a slice of Spam than fried crisp or in teriyaki sauce, atop a slab of sticky white rice, secured by a strip of nori? Spam *musubi* is a light meal or a snack, convenient to eat and tasty. It is found almost anywhere food-to-go is sold, and some of the best, embellished with other tasty ingredients, is found at golf course snack shops.

SUSHI

Sushi is ubiquitous in the islands and a great eat-on-the-go food. But local-style sushi is different from the variety found in sushi bars: the rice has a more pronounced vinegar-salt-sugar flavor, and inside a roll wrapped in seaweed are canned tuna, vegetables and shrimp flakes that are bright red or green. This is called "black" or *maki* sushi. *Inari* or cone sushi consists of seasoned rice with bits of carrot, green bean and *gobo* filling a triangular piece of *aburage*. There's no wasabi served with local sushi.

Sushi can be found in supermarkets, fast-stops at gas stations and just about everywhere local food is found. More and more you'll find the sushi bar varieties in these places too. The best local-style sushi is found in *okazu ya* (see page 26).

PASTELE

Pastele (pronounced pa-tel-lay) is a Puerto Rican version of a tamale. It is made with grated green banana, surrounding a savory filling of pork, green pepper, cilantro, olives, tomato sauce and seasonings. *Achiote*, or *annatto*, seeds, infused in oil, lend their color to the pastele. Served up hot, it's a savory, filling bundle of good flavor. Pastele are sold by roadside vendors and, best of all, made by Puerto Rican families and available at local festivals.

The Pastele Shop
2101 N. School St.
847-6969
Tues.-Sat. 10 a.m.-6 p.m.; Sun., Mon. 10 a.m.-5 p.m.
Parking available

HULI HULI CHICKEN

If you see a cloud of smoke billowing from a school or shopping center parking lot on a weekend, it's likely to be from a *huli huli* chicken sale. Halves of chicken, seasoned in a soy-based marinade, are cooked over *kiawe*-fired grills formed from recycled metal drums. School and charity groups sell the chicken, smoky and delicious, as a fund-raiser. *Huli* is Hawaiian for turn; *huli huli* chicken is turned many times during the cooking process. When you see the smoke, just drive up and grind.

MALASSADAS

Malassadas, deep-fried eggy doughnuts without a hole, coated in sugar, are borrowed from Portuguese cuisine and are best eaten hot, on the spot. *Malassadas* are Hawai'i's doughnut, better than a Krispy Kreme any day.

The Portuguese brought tempura to Japan, so it is no wonder

they brought the *malassada* to Hawai'i. There's even a special day for *malassadas* in Hawai'i: Shrove Tuesday, or Mardi Gras, the day before Ash Wednesday, the beginning of the Christian Lenten season, is known as Malassada Day. Used to be that Catholic Portuguese would use up their eggs and lard before Lent, and *malassadas* were a delicious way to do it.

Here again, creativity has taken hold, and you'll find *malassadas* stuffed with creamy fillings like *haupia*, chocolate, passion fruit curd or coffee cream. *Malassadas* are sometimes rolled in a mixture of sugar and *li hing mui* powder, too.

When it comes to *malassadas*, there are definite opinions as to who makes the best.

Agnes' Portuguese Bake Shop
46 Ho'olai St., Kailua
262-5367
Tues.-Sat. 6 a.m.-6 p.m.; Sun. 6 a.m.-2 p.m.; closed Mon.
Parking available

Although Agnes' is in Kailua, on the Windward side of O'ahu, not in Honolulu, no listing of places to get *malassadas* would be complete without this bakery that makes an old-fashioned *malassada* that's darned good.

Champion Malassadas
1926 S. Beretania St.
947-8778
Tues.-Sat. 6 a.m.-9 p.m.; Sun. 6:30 a.m.-7 p.m.; closed Mon.
Parking available

Owner Joc Miw came from Macao, once a Portuguese outpost in China. After years in Kalihi, he opened this location in 2000. Miw makes a *malassada* that's light, perhaps because of its longer rising time, which also results in a slightly tangy flavor. We also like the hot cross buns here.

Leonard's Bakery

933 Kapahulu Ave.
737-5591
Daily 6 a.m.-9 p.m.
Parking available

This is the home of the *malassada*, and aficionados will agree that it's tough to beat a Leonard's *malassada*: eggy flavor and good texture and always available hot. The Rego family set the standard and has made *malassadas* famous, selling them for over five decades. *Malassada* puffs filled with chocolate, custard and *haupia* are their newest innovation. *Pao duce*, a traditional Portuguese sweet bread, is also delicious here. You'll sometimes see a Leonard's red-and-white-striped *malassadas* wagon parked at supermarkets or at fairs—get a *malassada* while it's hot.

Punahou Carnival

Corner of Wilder and Punahou Streets
First Fri. and Sat. of February
944-5711

Each year in early February, people line up at the *malassada* booth at this annual school carnival to buy *malassadas* by the dozen. Made by volunteers (parents) who swear they'll never do it again, they're an honest, down-home treat you can't pass up. The carnival is also worth exploring for the different ethnic plates served up during the two-day event.

A N D A G I

Andagi is an Okinawan fried doughnut made with baking powder instead of yeast. Find these at ethnic festivals and craft fairs.

S N A C K   F O O D S

Crack Seed

Crack seed is Hawai'i's candy. Also known as *see mui*, these pre-served seasoned plums, cherries, peaches, apricots, mangoes and other fruit are imported from Asia, dried and seasoned with sugar, salt, star anise and other flavors. There are dozens of different crack seed varieties to choose from, each distinctive in flavor and texture.

Li hing mui, known as the traveler's plum, is the most distinguished and enduring variety of crack seed. It can be dry, wet or juicy, with or without a seed in the middle. It is sour, salty and sweet all at once, quite a jolt to the taste buds. The flavor is sold as a powder that can be applied to a variety of dried fruits and candies like gummi bears, mixed in ice cream and cakes and used in countless other ways. The *li hing mui* flavor figures prominently in today's sophisticated food scene. Don't be surprised to find a *li hing mui* vinaigrette, a *li hing mui* chutney served with foie gras, or *li hing mui* powder lacing a margarita glass.

Crack seed is an acquired taste if you haven't grown up on it. Start out with preserved apricots or rock salt plum; then make your way through the selections at the crack seed stores that are everywhere in Honolulu.

Crack Seed Center
Ala Moana Center
1450 Ala Moana Blvd.
949-7200
Mon.-Sat. 9:30 a.m.-9 p.m.; Sun. 10 a.m.-7 p.m.
Parking available
www. crackseedcenter.com

Crack Seed Store
1156 Koko Head Ave.
737-1022
Mon.-Sat. 9 a.m.-6:30 p.m.; Sun. noon-4:30 p.m.; closed last
    Sun. of month
Street parking

Kay's Crack Seed
Mānoa Marketplace
2752 Woodlawn Dr.
988-4338
Mon.-Fri. 9 a.m.-7 p.m.; Sat., Sun. 9 a.m.-6 p.m.
Parking available

Wholesale Unlimited and Wholesale Unlimited Express
960 Ahua St.
834-2900
Mon.-Fri. 8 a.m.-6 p.m.; Sat. 8 a.m.-4:30 p.m.; Sun. 10 a.m.-3
    p.m.
Parking available
Other locations downtown, Kāhala and Mānoa

Fruit Drinks

Local food veers to the salty side, so a sweet, refreshing drink is always in order. Guava, passion-guava, passion-orange-guava or *calamansi* drinks in cans are the drinks of choice in the islands, alongside the usual soda pops. Aloha Maid and Hawaiian Sun are the most ubiquitous brands, found everywhere soft drinks are sold.

Ice Cream

We all love good ice cream. Hawai'i has some special flavors that you won't find anywhere else: *haupia;* Kona coffee; guava, mango or passion fruit ice creams or sorbets; purple sweet potato; and macadamia nut, chock full of crunchy bits. And of course there's *mochi* ice cream, a bite-size dollop of flavored ice cream encased in a thin layer of rice cake. Locally made brands offer tropical flavors that Häagen-Dazs or Ben and Jerry's doesn't. Look for Roselani, Dave's, Tropilicious and La Gelateria in freezer cases of supermarkets, natural food stores and anywhere else ice cream is sold. Or go to one of these ice cream parlors:

Bubbie's
1010 University Ave.
949-8984
Mon.-Thurs. noon-midnight; Fri., Sat. noon-1 a.m.; Sun. noon-
    11:30 p.m.
Parking available

Koko Marina Shopping Center
396-8722
Sun.-Thurs. 10 a.m.-11 p.m.; Fri., Sat. 10 a.m.-midnight
Parking available

Dave's Hawaiian Ice Cream Parlors

611 Kapahulu Ave.
735-2194
Mon.-Sat. 1-10 p.m.; Sun. 1-5 p.m.
Parking available

Sears at Ala Moana Center
1450 Ala Moana Blvd.
944-9663
Mon.-Sat. 9:30 a.m.-9 p.m.; Sun. 10 a.m.-7 p.m.
Parking available

International Market Place
2330 Kalākaua Ave.
926-6104
Daily 10 a.m.-9 p.m.

Mochi

Mochi is a Japanese rice cake made with glutinous, or sweet, rice. This special rice is soaked, steamed, and then pounded into a thick, doughlike paste that is shaped into little cakes. There are traditional plain rice cakes, rather bland but soft and chewy, and those filled with sweetened *azuki* or lima beans. More recent versions have peanut butter or sweet potato fillings. There are versions of *mochi* made with butter, condensed milk, coconut milk or chocolate, and still others filled with ice cream. Some *mochi* is colored and flavored; some is eaten in soup, a tradition for the Japanese New Year celebration.

Mochi is eaten by everyone in Hawai'i, and almost every ethnic group makes a form of *mochi*. The Filipinos have their *bibing-ka;* the Koreans have their *duk* and *song pyun*; and the Chinese have their *gau*, a thick steamed cake made with brown sugar.

BUTTER *MOCHI*

Here's a basic *mochi* recipe that can be adapted to many flavors, each one delicious.

16 ounces glutinous rice flour
2 1/2 cups sugar
2 teaspoons baking powder
3 cups milk
1/2 cup butter, melted
4 eggs
2 teaspoons vanilla extract

Preheat oven to 350°.

In a bowl, mix together *mochi* rice flour, sugar and baking powder. In a large bowl, blend milk, butter, eggs and vanilla. Slowly add dry ingredients, whisking to incorporate into a smooth mixture. Add flavor additions, if desired.

Pour into 9x13-inch pan and bake for 60 minutes. Remove from oven, cool and cut into serving pieces.

Flavor additions:
- 1 cup shredded coconut
- 14-ounce can coconut milk; reduce milk to 1 1/2 cups
- 14-ounce can condensed milk; reduce milk to 1 1/2 cups
- 15-ounce can pumpkin purée and 2 teaspoons pumpkin pie spice
- 12 ounces semi sweet chocolate chips, melted

There is deep-fried poi, or taro, *mochi*, too. *Mochi* is a well-liked snack in the islands, so much so that there are cookbooks devoted to it. Find mochi at ethnic restaurants, supermarkets and just about everywhere in Honolulu. Or visit these factories:

Fujiya Limited

454 Waiakamilo Rd.
845-2921
Mon.-Fri. 7 a.m.-7:30 p.m.; Sat. 7 a.m.-2 p.m.
Parking available

Henry Onishi now owns this *mochi* shop that started over 50 years ago. From this kitchen come various *mochi,* steamed and baked *manju* with *azuki* bean or lima bean filling, *senbei,* and *yokan maki*, *azuki* beans wrapped in a cake layer. *Haupia* and blueberry *chichidango* are specialties. You can stop here to purchase or find their delicacies in supermarkets around Honolulu.

Nisshodo Candy Store

1095 Dillingham Blvd. Bldg. I-5
808 847-1244
Mon.-Fri. 7 a.m.-4 p.m.; Sat. 7 a.m.-3 p.m.; closed Sun.
Parking available

The Hirao family has been cooking up *mochi* treats since 1918, 18 years in the present location. The third generation has taken over, and this family-run business still puts out some of the best *chichidango*. It is also known for its *habutai, daifuku, tsumami* and peanut butter *mochi*. If it's Girls' Day (March 3), Boys' Day (May 5) or New Year's Day, this shop has the special *mochi* for that holiday. Nisshodo products are also found in supermarkets and stores throughout Honolulu.

Saloon Pilot Crackers

Saloon pilot crackers are round, firm, bland crackers that are like hardtack biscuits, which were a staple aboard sailing ships in the 1800s. They are, as they were back then, essentially a dry, crisp, hard, saltless bread that would last on long voyages. These crackers became part of the local diet and were eaten as a treat, often with guava jam or a drizzle of sweet condensed milk. *Kanaka* pudding is a treat of plantation days: a large, saloon pilot cracker, broken up into a bowl, sprinkled with sugar and drowned in evaporated milk or hot water. Find saloon pilot crackers in the cracker section of all food stores.

Shave Ice

Better than a snow cone, shave ice is perfect on a warm Hawaiian day. The finely shaved ice, achieved through a combination of perfect water freezing and a good ice shaver, is smothered in flavored syrup, strawberry being the flavor of choice for aficionados. The addition of sweetened *azuki* beans or a scoop of ice cream to the bottom of the cup is common and delicious. The whole experience of velvety ice on your tongue is sensational and so refreshing.

Halo halo is a Filipino version of shave ice. *Halo halo* is Tagalog for "mix mix"; it is a mixture of syrupy fruit, sweetened beans, coconut, sweet potato, rice and gelatin cubes, all mixed with shaved ice and drizzled with sweetened condensed milk or evaporated milk. It's a great concoction.

There's probably no better place in Honolulu to get a shave ice than Waiola Bakery and Shave Ice. Connoisseurs like the finely shaved ice, which feels silky smooth on the tongue, and the wonderful array of flavors. It's the best in Honolulu; only Matsumoto's and Aoki's, both in Hale'iwa, rival this one.

Waiola Bakery and Shave Ice

525 Kapahulu Ave.
735-8886
Daily 11 a.m.-6 p.m.
Street parking

Boiled Peanuts

Boiled peanuts are a tradition of the American South and no doubt made their way to the islands via a small band of southerners who came to work on the sugar plantations. Eating boiled peanuts is like eating boiled peas, since they are both legumes. Peanuts are soaked in salty water and boiled; they are delicious and very much considered a local treat.

HAWAIIAN FOOD

Hawaiian food is the food of native Hawaiians, a distinctive cuisine based on the foods brought here by Polynesian voyagers and others who have settled here over the years.

Hawai'i has a number of Hawaiian food restaurants, but Hawaiian food is at its best at a *lū'au*, a Hawaiian celebration that commemorates a birthday, marriage, graduation, anniversary or other important occasion with food and entertainment. Church *lū'au* are often open to the public; family *lū'au* are events that involve everyone in the preparation as well as the eating. Poi suppers are another form of *lū'au*, usually for a smaller gathering of people.

Lū'au tables are always lined with ti leaves and set with sweet onions and Hawaiian salt (see page 167), chili pepper water (see page 11), fresh pineapple, and coconut cake. Almost every *lū'au* menu is the same or at least features the following favorite items.

TARO AND POI

Taro is the starch staple of the traditional Hawaiian diet. It is steamed or baked and eaten like potatoes. The corm, or root, of the wetland variety is steamed and then pounded into a smooth paste called poi.

Fresh poi is very bland; one-day-old or two-day-old poi has a desirable sour tang. Poi's thickness, adjusted by the amount of water added to the pounded taro, is measured as one, two or three-finger poi; the thinner it is the more fingers required to bring it to the mouth.

Poi and taro are used as ingredients in baked goods like breads, biscuits, pancakes and even cheesecakes, adding a purple-gray cast to the finished product. Dryland varieties of taro are made into chips or used like potatoes.

KĀLUA PORK

The centerpiece of Hawaiian celebrations, *kālua* pork is well-cooked roasted pork, smoky and salty, like a pulled pork of the South or *carnitas* in Mexican cuisine. Traditionally it is cooked in an *imu*: a whole pig is placed in a pit surrounded by and filled with hot rocks, covered with banana and ti leaves and smoldered for several hours. When the pig is cooked, the meat is removed from the carcass, shredded and served. Home cooks often prepare *kālua* using pork butts seasoned with salt and liquid smoke, roasted for a few hours in an oven.

Kālua pork is eaten alongside poi and *lomi lomi* salmon—a trilogy of Hawaiian food that is a must for food lovers. *Kālua pork* is used in preparations like *quesadillas*, *enchiladas*, breakfast hash, omelets and salads or cooked with cabbage. It is available at supermarkets as well as at Hawaiian food markets and restaurants.

LOMI LOMI SALMON

To make *lomi lomi* salmon, raw, salted salmon is diced and combined with tomatoes and sweet onions to form a salad of sorts. *Lomi lomi* means to work with the fingers, which is how this mixture is prepared. Salted salmon was introduced to the islands by whale-hunting Russian sailors who stopped in Hawai'i in the 1800s to replenish their supplies.

POKE

Poke means to cut into small pieces. This Hawaiian word, pronounced *po-keh*, is used mostly to describe a dish of bite-size pieces of seasoned fish or seafood. Traditionally, Hawaiians cut

OVEN *KĀLUA* PORK

Kālua pork is one of Hawai'i's favorite foods. The well-cooked, smoky and well-seasoned pork is perfect with rice, or eat it with poi and *lomi* salmon. Use *kālua* pork as a filling for tacos or quesadillas. Or cook up one of Hawai'i's favorite dishes, *kālua* pork and cabbage.

aluminum foil
6 to 8 ti leaves
4- to 5-pound pork butt
2 tablespoons Hawaiian salt
3 tablespoons liquid smoke

Preheat oven to 325°. Place a large piece of aluminum foil in a roasting pan. Arrange ti leaves on top of foil. Place pork on ti leaves. Rub salt into pork roast. Sprinkle liquid smoke over pork and rub into pork. Fold ti leaves to wrap pork and wrap the bundle in foil. Place in oven for 4 to 5 hours. Unwrap and shred meat to serve. Serves 8 to 10.

Kālua Pork and Cabbage: Sauté one onion and sliced head cabbage in 2 tablespoons of oil. Cook until wilted and add 2 cups shredded *kālua* pork. Mix and simmer for 15 minutes. Season to taste with soy sauce or salt. Serve with rice.

their raw fish into pieces and seasoned it with salt, seaweed and *inamona*. In the 1970s, fish stores began cutting up their *'ahi* trimmings and seasoning them with soy sauce, garlic, ginger, sesame and green onions. Since then, *poke* has been a popular dish to eat with a pair of chopsticks, accompanied by a cold beer or glass of wine. *Poke* can be made with fish, octopus, squid, crab, lobster, clams or even tofu; there are probably two dozen different types of *poke* made. It is Hawai'i's favorite *pūpū*—hors d'oeuvre— bar none, enjoyed at home, at the beach, at hole-in-the-wall restaurants and fine-dining venues. It is available at supermarkets, fish stores and Hawaiian food markets.

L Ū ʻ A U

The word *lūʻau* refers to the celebration meal but also to the leafy tops of the taro plant. *Lūʻau* are cooked into a rich stew with bits of squid or chicken and flavored with coconut milk. They are also used to make *lau lau*. Taro leaves must be cooked thoroughly before eating; otherwise, calcium oxalate crystals will irritate the mouth.

LAU LAU

To make *lau lau*, *lū'au*, pork and salted butterfish are wrapped in ti leaves and steamed to form a meal in a bundle. Chicken and turkey are also used to make *lau lau*; all types can be found at supermarkets and Hawaiian food markets and restaurants.

CHICKEN LONG RICE

Chicken long rice consists of Chinese mung bean threads or rice vermicelli cooked with chicken, ginger and green onions in a souplike preparation. This dish reflects the influx of ingredients from other parts of the world into Hawai'i.

PIPIKAULA

Pipikaula is dried beef, seasoned with salt or soy, perhaps a little chili pepper. It's Hawai'i's version of beef jerky, though more tender and savory.

'ŌPIHI

'Ōpihi is a Hawaiian limpet harvested from rocky coastlines and eaten raw. It tastes of the sea, clean and briny.

SWEET POTATO

'Uala, the sweet potato, was the second most important food source for early Hawaiians. Steamed or baked sweet potatoes are a part of every *lū'au* menu. White, yellow and purple (also known as Okinawan) varieties are popular here.

KŪLOLO

Kūlolo is a baked or steamed pudding made of grated taro and coconut cream. Sweet and chewy, it has a brownish-purplish color that makes it appear rather suspect, but it is quite delicious.

HAUPIA

Haupia is a creamy coconut pudding made of coconut milk thickened with arrowroot or cornstarch. Island bakeries layer cakes with *haupia* or combine it with chocolate, pumpkin or sweet potato in pies.

HAUPIA

A simple and delicious sweet treat, *haupia* is loved by all. Eat it as is, use it to fill cake layers or layer it with sweet potato in a pie.

1 14-ounce can coconut milk
2 tablespoons sugar
2 tablespoons cornstarch
Pinch of salt

Heat 1 cup of coconut milk in a saucepan. While milk is heating, whisk together remaining coconut milk, sugar, cornstarch and salt. When milk is just about to boil, add milk mixture and whisk together. Lower heat and simmer for about 2 minutes. Pour mixture into an 8x8-inch pan. Cool to room temperature, cover and refrigerate. To serve, remove from refrigerator, cut into serving size pieces and serve.

WHERE TO FIND HAWAIIAN FOOD

All of the following Hawaiian food places have been in business for decades, attesting to the popularity of Hawaiian food and the good food that is served in each place.

Haili's Hawaiian Food
Ward Farmers' Market
1020 'Auahi St.
593-8019
Mon.-Sat. 7:30 a.m.-4:30 p.m.; Sun. 7:30 a.m.-1 p.m.
Parking available

Over 50 years old, this Hawaiian takeout spot continues to provide great food at reasonable prices. The Haili family continues to produce good Hawaiian fare, and they have a fine reputation as a *lū'au* caterer. This is strictly a food-to-go place.

Helena's Hawaiian Food
1240 N. School St.
Tues.-Fri. 10 a.m.-7:30 p.m., closed Sat., Sun., Mon.
845-8044
Parking available; street parking

Named as one of America's regional classic restaurants by the James Beard Foundation in 2000, Helena's is known for its *pipikaula*-style short ribs, *kālua* pork and cabbage, squid *lū'au* and other Hawaiian comfort foods. Helena Chock has been preparing Hawaiian food for over 60 years; her grandson Craig Katsuyoshi continues the tradition of satisfying cravings for Hawaiian food.

Ono Hawaiian Foods
726 Kapahulu Ave.
737-2275
Mon.-Sat. 11 a.m.-7:45 p.m.; closed Sun.
Street parking

The snaking line attests to the popularity of this Hawaiian food restaurant that has been in business for at least 40 years. Sueko Oh Young was the founder and cook; her family continues the delicious tradition. *Kālua pork*, *lau lau*, chicken long rice or combination plates get you a taste of everything. Order à la carte, too.

Young's Fish Market
City Square Shopping Center
1286 Kalani St.
841-4885
Mon.-Fri. 8 a.m.-5 p.m.; Sat. 8 a.m.-4 p.m.; closed Sun.
Parking available

The best place to get *lau lau* and some of the best *kālua* pork in town made in a traditional *imu*. Enjoy a Hawaiian plate on the premises or take it home; if you're traveling you'll find frozen *lau lau, kālua* pork, and other items, ready to pack and go.

FISH AND SEAFOOD

Lucky you live Hawai'i when it comes to fresh fish. Surrounded by water, we take for granted that we'll find fish every day at our supermarkets, fish markets, neighborhood grocery stores, restaurants and eateries.

The Hawai'i Regional Cuisine (see page 73) chefs made local fish the center of the plate starting in the late 1980s. As a result, the fishing industry has been busy and more fish are available for everyone to enjoy. Deep-water 'ahi, served mostly raw or seared (rare) is perhaps the most popular of fish in Hawai'i. Mahimahi, too, is a staple of the table. Fish like 'ōpakapaka and onaga, often seen on the menus of top restaurants, are becoming scarce and their prices are high. That's all the more reason to try some of the many other species harvested from our island Pacific waters.

Spiny lobsters and deep-water shrimp are seasonal and not plentiful around the islands. Between September and April, Kona crabs are in season. Also known as the red frog crab, the Kona crab is found in wide sandy areas near Kīhei on Maui, Kona on Hawai'i and Waikīkī on O'ahu. This bright-orange crab has short, flat legs and not-very-large claws protruding from each side of a squarish body. It's a hard-shelled crab that turns red orange when cooked. Inside is sweet, delicate, but firm meat that requires patience and diligence to retrieve. Steaming it is the best way to prepare it; restaurants sometimes feature Kona crab cakes.

BUYING FRESH FISH

To be certain you're getting fresh, not frozen, fish, get to know your fishmonger. Be it at a supermarket or a store specializing in seafood, learn to trust the proprietor to tell you what's good. It's not just a matter of age, but quality too.

For example, 'ahi, prized for sashimi, is priced according to its quality. The higher the price, the better the sashimi will be, firm but oily, not too fishy. But one fishmonger's best 'ahi might be another's lowest quality. If that 'ahi is bright red, it might have been treated with carbon monoxide, to preserve its color and fresh looks. If that 'ahi is soft to the touch, it is likely too old for good eating. Smell fishy? Better to find another piece of fish.

Packaged fish should always be cold to the touch; refrigeration is key to maintaining the quality of fresh fish. Always check the bloodline, the dark strip in a fish steak. If it is bright red, the fish is fresh; darker, the fish is starting to age.

FISH TASTES AND TEXTURES

'Ahi/Bigeye tuna: deep red flesh with high fat content, firm texture and gutsy flavor. Best served raw or rare, preferred for sashimi and *poke*.

'Ahi/Yellowfin tuna: deep red flesh with high fat content, steak-like texture and beefy flavor. Best served raw or rare, preferred for sashimi and *poke*.

'Ahi tombo/Albacore tuna: light pink flesh, firm but fine texture, full flavored with a slight tang. A premium canned product; best grilled or used in soups and pasta dishes.

Aku/Skipjack tuna: deep red firm flesh with a bold, acidic flavor, dense and meaty. Used in raw preparations like *poke* or *tataki*.

Kajiki/A'u, or Pacific blue marlin: amber flesh that cooks to white; can be fibrous and chewy; firm with a mild-to-medium flavor intensity. A favorite of sport fishermen; best cooked.

Mahimahi/Dolphinfish, or dorado: Thin-skinned fish with firm, light pink flesh that is mellow, meaty and silky. An all-time island favorite, grilled, sautéed, baked or steamed; occasionally served raw.

Whole fish should have clear, not cloudy eyes, and red color in the gills. The flesh should feel firm and it should smell of the ocean, not fishy.

AQUACULTURE PRODUCTS

At Keāhole Point, south of the Kona airport on the island of Hawai'i, lies the Natural Energy Laboratory, where mineral-rich ocean water from depths of 2,000 feet is pumped to the surface.

Monchong/**Bigscale, or sickle, pomfret:** Clear white flesh with pink tones, firm in texture, with high fat content; medium flavored. Excellent for grilling or steaming.

Nairage/A'u, **or striped marlin:** light pink flesh, medium-firm texture with a medium-intensity refined flavor. Best eating of the marlin species; prepare on a grill or raw.

Onaga/**Red snapper:** sweet, mild-flavored, delicate flesh that has a melt-in-your-mouth quality. Steaming is the preferred preparation; raw is good, too.

Ono/**Wahoo:** white flaky flesh that is firm with a moderate intensity. This relative of the king mackerel is well suited to steaming or poaching.

Opah/Moonfish: large-grained flesh that is rich and fatty, with full flavor and soft texture. Holds up well in soups and stews.

'Ōpakapaka/**Pink snapper:** light pink flesh that is firm, smooth and mild. Sauté, steam or bake, *'ōpakapaka* is Hawai'i's premier fish.

Shutome/**Swordfish:** sweet, mild flavor with a succulent, meaty texture owing to its high fat content. Excellent grilled; comparable to Atlantic swordfish.

The cold water is used to air-condition the facility and, more important, produce food in a variety of applications.

Nutritional supplements processed from algae are grown here; shrimp brood stock is shipped internationally for grow-out, and clams in the Pacific Northwest begin their life in this nutrient-rich water. Maine lobsters are kept alive and well fed in this cold water to be shipped to restaurants throughout the state; seaweed is grown to feed abalone that ends up in sushi bars here and in Japan, and experiments are ongoing in the production of other food products using this ocean resource.

Throughout the state, aquaculture products are finding their way from small and large venues to restaurants and retail stores. Catfish, tilapia (also known as sunfish), *awa* (milkfish), grass carp, shrimp and prawns (in Hawai'i we refer to shrimp as saltwater creatures and prawns as freshwater creatures) are often found in

Chinatown markets or fish markets throughout Honolulu, all raised in earth-based ponds.

Moi, a delicate white fish once reserved for Hawaiian royalty, is being raised in open ocean cages submerged 40 feet below the surface off the south shore of Oʻahu. A one-pound fish, perfect for one serving, is very popular among diners in Honolulu restaurants as well as among home cooks. *Kampachi*, an oily fish akin to *hamachi* that is popular in sushi bars, is being grown in open ocean cages at Keāhole, following the lead of the *moi* farmers.

Limu, edible seaweed, is another product of aquaculture. Once an integral part of the native Hawaiian diet, *ogo,* as it is also known, is harvested at the shoreline and is rich in complex carbohydrates and protein, low in calories and a good source of vitamin A, calcium and potassium. This crunchy, hairlike seaweed is often used in *poke* preparations or blanched and dressed like a salad.

Fort Ruger Market

3585 Alohea Avenue
737-4531
Mon.-Sat. 6:30 a.m. - 6 p.m., Sun. 6:30 a.m. -4:30 p.m.
Parking available; also street parking

Tucked in a residential area, this small market specializes in takeout foods amid its shelves of groceries, beer and wine. It is best known for its *poke*, made fresh to order. *Poke* sitting in soy sauce for many hours is just not as good as freshly mixed, and besides, you get to season *poke* to your liking. Hawaiian food plates and beef stew are also well liked here, as are the boiled peanuts. Bradley and Loren Pulice are the owners, having taken over this gem of a food stop from its original owner five years ago.

POKE

Hawai'i's most ubiquitous *pūpū, poke* is found everywhere food is sold and eaten at just about any event. It's fresh, it's delicious and it's unique to Hawai'i.

1 pound *'ahi*
1/2 cup chopped *limu*
1/2 cup sliced sweet onion
1 fresh chili pepper or 1/2 teaspoon crushed red pepper
1/2 cup soy sauce
1 clove garlic, finely minced
1 teaspoon ginger, finely minced
1/4 cup finely chopped green onions
1 tablespoon honey
1 tablespoon sesame oil

Cut *'ahi* into 1/2-inch cubes. Place in a bowl with *limu*, onion and chili pepper.

In a small bowl, whisk together the remaining ingredients. Pour over *'ahi* and mix well. Serve immediately. Serves 6 to 8 as an appetizer.

Honolulu Fish Auction
Pier 38 off Nimitz Hwy.
Daily except Sun. from 5:30 a.m.
Parking available

Hawai'i's only fish auction and perhaps one of a few left in the United States today, the Honolulu Fish Auction, conducted by United Fishing Agency, convenes in the early morning hours as fishing boats tie up to the dock at Pier 38. Thousands of pounds of just-caught fish are auctioned each morning to fish retailers, wholesalers, distributors and brokers who buy for Honolulu fish stores, supermarkets, restaurants and mainland and international markets.

Hawai'i's longline fishing fleet ventures hundreds of miles away from the islands in pursuit of *'ahi, tombo 'ahi, aku* and

swordfish. While they tend their lines, they'll also catch marlin, opah, *monchong,* mahimahi, *onaga, 'ōpakapaka* and other tasty fish. After a day or up to ten days, boats come ashore at Pier 38 to unload their catch at the auction house, where the fish are weighed, tagged, iced and placed on pallets for fish buyers to view.

It's a sight to see as a small crowd of buyers hovers around the auctioneer, moving up and down rows and rows of fish on pallets. Fish are auctioned one by one in increments of 10 cents per pound. Quality is the primary consideration as these experienced buyers bid according to their customers' requirements.

Individuals can buy fish here, too, assuming they want a whole fish (tuna can weigh well over a hundred pounds) and can manage to filet it (all the fish are gutted on the ocean). Most of us rely on our favorite fish store or supermarket for portion-size pieces, ready to cook, knowing that we have access to some of the freshest fish on earth.

Visitors are welcome at the fish auction. It's best to go early in the morning, since one never knows how long the auction will last—that depends on how many boats are in and how much they've caught. Do wear long pants and covered shoes (rubber soles are best, since the area is wet) and a light jacket or sweater. The beehive of activity requires that you stand on the side and walk carefully, but there's always someone around who can tell you what kind of fish you're facing.

During the week between Christmas and New Year's Day, the fish auction starts at 3:30 a.m. The demand for *'ahi* sashimi fuels this activity as well as higher prices for good-quality tuna. But no matter what time of year, the Honolulu fish auction is always an interesting adventure for food lovers.

Nico's at Pier 38
1133 Nimitz Hwy.
540-1377
Mon.-Sat. 6:30 a.m.-2:30 p.m.
Parking available

Just in case you get a little hungry for fish, walk next door to Pacific Ocean Producers, where Nico's at Pier 38 can satisfy your appetite. Nicholas Chaize is the owner/chef here, far from his home in Lyon, France. But he's right at home at the pier where Honolulu's fishing fleet pulls up with their fresh catch. Having the freshest fish cooked up into a tasty meal is the reason folks like this casual dining spot. You can't go wrong with a breakfast of fish, eggs and fried rice to start your day or lunch prepared with a French flair. Of course, there are also local favorites like beef stew and teriyaki, all served up in Styrofoam containers as you sit at plastic tables overlooking the harbor.

Tamashiro Market

802 N. King St.
841-8047
Mon.-Fri. 9 a.m.-6 p.m.; Sat. 8 a.m.-6 p.m.; Sun. 8 a.m.-4 p.m.
Parking available; also across street at Kaumakapili Church

The third generation of the Tamashiro family runs this small but very efficient neighborhood grocery store in the Kalihi area of Honolulu. Tamashiro's has been here for more than half a century and it is renowned for its fish and seafood. If there's anything you want from the water world, you're likely to find it here, fresh, frozen or dried. Especially wonderful is the selection of fresh-caught fish from Hawaiian waters, from the pelagic tunas and marlins to the bottom-dwelling snappers and mahimahi to the small reef fish that are caught along O'ahu's shorelines. What's nice is that the fishmongers will clean and filet fish for you; of course larger fish are blocked and cut to your specifications.

Water-filled tanks house live lobsters, crab and shrimp; freezers offer soft-shell crabs, squid, shrimp and seafood from international locales; icy beds keep clams, oysters, mussels and other items fresh. *Limu* and aquacultured fish and shrimp are available here, too. When it's time to make a *bouillabaisse* or *paella* and you need a variety of seafood, this is the place to come.

Tamashiro's is also known for its wide array of *poke*—seasoned bite-size morsels of seafood—made with the freshest of *'ahi, tako,* mussels, crab and other seafood delicacies. At least two dozen varieties are made fresh daily here, along with other prepared foods like boiled sweet potatoes, sushi and Spam *musubi*.

Specialty items like quail eggs, *tobiko*, *ikura* and sometimes fresh wasabi can be found here. But for all of its delicacies, Tamashiro's is also a neighborhood grocery store that serves its nearby community of South Pacific islanders and Filipinos. Such local items as breadfruit, taro and ti leaves and a full array of meats and vegetables are displayed in this small but well-stocked store. During mango season it's the best place to find green mangoes for pickling and chutney making and good ripe mangoes of various varieties.

HAWAI‘I REGIONAL CUISINE RESTAURANTS

Fine dining in Honolulu got finer in the 1990s as French- and American-trained chefs began marrying Asian flavors and techniques with classic haute cuisine. They added fresh vegetables and fruits raised right here in the islands to create Hawai‘i Regional Cuisine, which was well received by food lovers in Hawai‘i.

Today's restaurant scene is exciting for its joining of island products and local flavors with sophisticated presentations and refined techniques. There's definitely an Asian bent to most of the restaurants listed here, but each one is distinctively different once you understand the chef's background and training. These are the restaurants you go to knowing that you'll always dine well and it will be worth every penny.

3660 on the Rise

3600 Wai‘alae Ave.
737-1177
Dinner Tues.-Sun. from 5:30 p.m., last order at 8:30 p.m.;
    closed Mon.
Parking in building and on street
www.3660.com

Island-born-and-raised chef Russell Siu has been serving up a wonderful blend of Euro-Asian cuisine at this popular neighborhood bistro since 1992. With partner Gale Ogawa, who greets you at the door, Siu has maintained a menu of consistent quality and good flavors that relies on locally grown food products served in a setting with a warm, casual ambiance.

Siu learned to cook at the side of his Chinese grandfather; his "Betty Crocker" mom taught him to bake even before he learned to cook. No wonder the desserts here are always terrific. But before dessert you'll want to try Siu's *'ahi katsu*, the best *'ahi* preparation in Honolulu, bar none. Potato-crusted crab cakes, clam and corn chowder, New York steak *'alaea* and tempura catfish are some of the signature dishes. And of course, there's always steamed fish, usually snapper, prepared in a Chinese black bean broth. Vegetarian items are highlighted each day.

Siu likes to feature seasonal items like Copper River salmon and soft-shell crabs when they are fresh. Wine dinners and cooking classes, as well as martini nights and entertainment in the restaurant's banquet room, are part of the restaurant's many events. Private dinners are always possible.

What's best about 3660 on the Rise is that you always know you'll find something tempting on the menu and that it will more than live up to your expectations.

Alan Wong's

1857 S. King St.
949-2526
Dinner daily from 5 p.m.; last seating at 9 p.m.
Valet parking, street parking
www.alanwongs.com

The perennial award-winning restaurant in Honolulu is Alan Wong's and for good reasons: excellent food and service. Chef Alan Wong, James Beard Foundation Best Chef, Pacific Northwest/Hawai'i 1996 award winner, grew up in Hawai'i, learned basic culinary skills here, and then went on to apprentice at the Greenbrier Hotel in West Virginia and at Andre Soltner's Lutèce restaurant in New York City. When Wong returned to the islands, he was well grounded in the craft of cooking, which he then married with his local upbringing.

What emerged was a repertoire of local and ethnic dishes

elevated to the realm of fine dining. *Poke* is wrapped in crisp won ton strips to create Poki-Pines; tomatoes are served with *li hing mui* vinaigrette, and lamb chops are coated in macadamia nuts and coconut. Fresh tomato soup and a *kālua* pork, cheese and foie gras sandwich is the ultimate "soup and sandwich." The flavors are essentially Asian, the ingredients as fresh and locally produced as one can get and the presentations spectacular. And it's all put together with a sense of humor that makes eating it lots of fun and most definitely satisfying.

Save room for dessert at Alan Wong's: pastry chef Mark Okumura's Five Spoonfuls of Brulée, Chocolate Crunch Bars, and Coconut are incredibly wonderful. Pineapple martinis will get your meal off to a good start, and there's an excellent wine list here, too.

Wong was among the dozen Hawai'i Regional Cuisine chefs that synthesized the elements involved in creating great food based on local ingredients and put Hawai'i on the map of good cuisine. His culinary excellence emerged at the Canoe House at the Mauna Lani Bay Hotel on the island of Hawai'i, and since 1995 his award-winning namesake restaurant continues to pack in residents and visitors alike. Alan Wong's is a must for food lovers who want to understand the trajectory of local food, past, present and future.

Alan Wong's Pineapple Room

Macy's at Ala Moana Center
1450 Ala Moana Blvd.
945-6573
Lunch Mon.-Fri. 11 a.m.-3:30 p.m., Sat. 11:15 a.m.-3:30 p.m.,
    Sun. 11:15 a.m.-3 p.m.
Dinner Mon.-Sat. from 4 p.m.; last order at 8:30 p.m.
Parking available
www.alanwongs.com

This is Chef Alan Wong's second restaurant, located within Macy's Ala Moana Center department store, where shoppers stop for lunch or treat themselves to dinner before heading home. It's easier to get dinner reservations here than at Wong's King St. location, but the menu is decidedly different. At both locations, comforting soul food, based on local flavors and foods, is what Wong is all about. Wong has quite a repertoire of these dishes, so he serves some at the Pineapple Room and others at King St.

Chef Neil Nakasone has been working alongside Wong for many years, so he knows well the "Wong Way" of doing things. Try a poi cup: *kālua* pork and *lomi* tomato with fresh poi. While you're having a beer or sipping wine from the extensive list, pop a few finger-licking-good stir-fried soybeans with chilis, garlic and soy sesame sauce. A Thai Cobb salad, *kālua* pork BLT, meat loaf, crab cakes—they're all delicious. And don't forget pastry chef Mark Okumura's desserts.

Chai's Island Bistro

Aloha Tower Marketplace
585-0011
Lunch Tues.-Fri. 11 a.m.-4 p.m. Dinner daily 4-10 p.m.
Validated parking in Marketplace
www.chaisislandbistro.com

When Chai Chaowasaree came to Honolulu, he opened Singha Thai Cuisine, in Waikīkī. A Thai menu, Thai dancers, a profusion of orchids and a fine Thai dining experience made it a successful venture. But the chef wanted to be more creative, blending new taste experiences with those from his Southeast Asian background. So in 1999 Chai's Island Bistro was born, enticing diners with contemporary Pacific Rim food that has garnered rave reviews and awards.

Thai influences on the menu are evident, with lemongrass, chili, peanut *saté* and coconut figuring in some of the dishes. But the food is mostly about what the chef likes: prawns encrusted in crisp fried *kataifi*, spring rolls filled with duck confit, *moi* steamed with Asian pesto and sake. It's a savory blend of East and West served in a lush indoor-outdoor atmosphere. Colorful paintings by Fabienne Blanc adorn the walls, orchids are profusely displayed and waiters snappily serve you. In the evening, Chai's becomes an entertainment venue featuring some of the finest musicians in Hawai'i. What could be better than to listen to the Brothers Cazimero while having dinner?

Chef Mavro

1969 S. King St.
944-4714
Dinner Tues.-Sun. from 6 p.m.; last seating at 9:30 p.m.
Valet parking
www.chefmavro.com

When it comes to fine French food, Chef Mavro restaurant is easily at the top of its game. The meticulous chef, George Mavrothalissitis, spares neither a dime nor time in the preparation of dishes for his menu. He has befriended dozens of farmers, fishermen and other food purveyors in the pursuit of the best and freshest of ingredients. Then he insists on a step-by-step controlled preparation of these ingredients that results in dishes of simplicity that belie all the work that went into them. This is clean, delicious food without a lot of frou frou and with a whole lot of elegance. Be sure to try his salt-baked *onaga*, available only by special request, and *liliko'i malassadas*, a fine tribute to a local favorite.

On top of that, the chef takes wine seriously and pairs each dish with a wine. Each quarter, as he prepares to launch his seasonal menu, the chef gathers his staff to taste the upcoming dishes and possible wine selections. It's a democratic process and one that is unique among restaurateurs.

Mavrothalassitis was one of the founding Hawai'i Regional Cuisine chefs and, more noteworthy, the 2003 James Beard Foundation award winner for the Pacific Northwest/Hawai'i region. Originally from Marseilles, France, he came to the islands in 1988, wooed by the sand and surf as so many other European-trained chefs have been, to work in the hotel industry. Mavrothalassitis earned his stars at the Halekūlani in Waikīkī and the Four Seasons on Maui before opening his 60-seat restaurant in 1998.

Hiroshi's Eurasian Tapas

Restaurant Row
500 Ala Moana Blvd.
533-4476
Dinner daily 5:30-9:30 p.m.
Validated parking

Japanese-trained chef Hiroshi Fukui doesn't say much, but his food speaks volumes. It is a fusion of Japan and the West, with soy sauce and butter marrying well on the plate.

Fukui built his reputation at L'Uraku, where his contemporary blend of Japanese flavors and techniques with island-grown products earned him accolades in the food press, locally and nationally. In 2004 he decided to move on and partnered with D. K. Kodama of Sansei to open a restaurant inspired by Asian and European flavors. In his own place he experiments with new techniques like foams and includes more ingredients in his repertoire, like kalamata olives and Parmesan cheese with *sashimi*!

You might think the food is contrived, but it's not. Traditional Japanese dishes like *chazuke* are given a twist, highlighting their simplicity but showing a layer of complexity. Braised veal cheeks are simply excellent. Master sommelier Chuck Furuya oversees the wine list, which is masterfully paired to the nuances of Fukui's food.

A couple of times a year, Fukui presents a contemporary *kaiseki* dinner, a multicourse tasting affair following the traditional *kaiseki* format but infused with his creative flair. It's usually an amazing evening of food.

Hoku's

Kāhala Mandarin Oriental Hawai'i
5000 Kāhala Ave.
739-8888
Lunch Mon.-Fri. 11:30 a.m.-2 p.m.
Dinner nightly 5:30-10 p.m.
Sunday brunch 10:30 a.m.-2 p.m.
Validated and valet parking

Hotel restaurants are rarely as good as Hoku's. Executive Chef Wayne Hirabayashi serves fresh island products in a sophisticated and elegant way with wonderful casualness on the plate.

A tandoori oven turns out pillows of naan and *ciabatta* bread served with an 'ahi dip that's so delicious you could make it a meal. The 'ahi poke musubi on the dinner menu will make you a fan for life. Whole snappers are deep-fried and presented for eating with sauces in a spectacular presentation. The seafood tower is equally eye popping. The flavors are simple, spanning the eastern and western worlds, and the preparations expertly executed. And you can watch it all happen in the exhibition kitchen.

Island-born Hirabayashi expanded his palette in Singapore and other parts of Asia and his experience and love of local food are evident in his preparations. Hoku's is among Honolulu's finest dining spots, with a wine list and service to match.

Le Bistro

5730 Kalaniana'ole Hwy.
373-7990
Dinner nightly except Tues. from 5:30 p.m.
Parking available

Le Bistro has become a favorite East Honolulu dining spot since its opening in 2001. It's just a neighborhood bistro, really, but a fine one.

Chef Alan Takasaki and his wife, Debbie, work in tandem, he in the kitchen and she up front, to provide good food and good service, both at good prices. The flavors here are earthy and savory, with an inventive touch. Must-try dishes: greens topped with gorgonzola and pear; braised short ribs flavored with honey and balsamic vinegar, spaghettini with gorgonzola and slivered almonds, and just about every fish and seafood preparation.

Takasaki is well traveled and well versed in culinary basics from stints in New Orleans, New York, Los Angeles and other spots in Honolulu. His well-grounded palate is refreshingly western-focused, as a good bistro should be.

Mariposa
Neiman Marcus at Ala Moana Center
1450 Ala Moana Blvd.
951-3420
Lunch Mon.-Sat., Sun. brunch 11 a.m.-3 p.m.
Appetizers and cocktails daily 3-5 p.m.
Dinner nightly 5-9 p.m.; Thurs.-Sat. until 10 p.m.
Parking available; also valet parking

Housed in a tony department store, Mariposa offers light and elegant fare and a terrific view of Ala Moana Beach Park. Chef Doug Lum is an islander who spent several years cooking on the mainland before doing stints in a couple of renowned restaurants in the islands. He has hit his stride at Mariposa (he also oversees two other food operations in the store), offering some nice salads, sandwiches and entrées for the mostly shopping crowd. Lobster *katsu* with mango lime dipping sauce is certainly a winner; there are standard Neiman Marcus menu items here, too. Mariposa is a nice refuge from the frenzied activity of Ala Moana Center.

On Jin's Cafe

401 Kamakee St.
589-1666
Lunch daily 11 a.m.-4 p.m.
Dinner Sun.-Thurs. 4-9 p.m.; Fri., Sat. 4-10 p.m.
Parking available and on street

Plate lunches by day, fine dining at night is this restaurant's operational mode. But all of it is fine in terms of food. Chef/owner On Jin Kim's Korean palate inspires some incredible combinations like *pul ko gi* and kim chee sandwiches, *'ahi don* (sashimi atop Nalo greens) with *ko chu jang* sauce, and popular *kal bi*. For dinner you can't beat her charred *'ahi* with *liliko'i* beurre blanc or lobster ravioli with vanilla sauce. It's all nicely done in a cozy, comfortable ambiance.

Orchids

Halekūlani Hotel
2199 Kālia Road
923-2311
Breakfast Mon.-Sat. 7:30-11 a.m.;
Sunday brunch 9:30 a.m.-2:30 p.m. Lunch daily 11:30
    a.m.-2 p.m.
Dinner daily 6-10 p.m.
Valet parking

Unlike the formal La Mer dining room upstairs, this dining venue alongside Waikīkī Beach is very elegant in a casual way. Darryl Fujita, executive chef of the hotel, personally oversees the kitchen, adding his love of things local to a menu that has to appeal to sophisticated world travelers as well as the businesspeople and other local folks who like to dine here. Service is impeccable: this is the Halekūlani, after all, known for its fine service, and you can't beat the picturesque oceanside people-and-surf watching. Try the steamed *onaga*, prepared Chinese-style with soy sauce, ginger and garlic, perfect every time. Seafood is always a winner here.

Roy's
6600 Kalaniana'ole Hwy.
396-7697
Dinner Sun.-Thurs. from 5:30 p.m., last seating 9 p.m.; Fri. last
    seating at 9:30 p.m.; Sat. from 5 p.m., last seating 9:30
    p.m.
Parking available
www.roysrestaurant.com

The award-winning Roy's is the flagship restaurant of a restaurant empire (over 30 restaurants in 2005) that started in 1988 in the East Honolulu suburb of Hawai'i Kai. Roy Yamaguchi, its founder, grew up in Japan but spent summers with grandparents on Maui. His interest in food led him to the Culinary Institute of America in New York and on to Los Angeles, where he became the first chef on record to fuse European techniques with Asian ingredients.

Yamaguchi's Hawaiian fusion cuisine began the blending of East and West that is so prevalent in Hawai'i and throughout the world. His is a bold cuisine, rooted in Japanese, Thai, Chinese, Singaporean, Korean and Malaysian ingredients married to European and American techniques. Signature dishes include blackened *'ahi*, Szechwan spiced baby back ribs, Hawai'i-style *misoyaki* butterfish, and melting chocolate soufflé. Oh yes, and his meat loaf.

Roy's is a casual family dining kind of place that's definitely more upscale than a cafe or bistro. Yamaguchi is one of the Hawai'i Regional Cuisine chefs and winner of the 1993 Best Chef

Pacific Northwest/Hawai'i award from the James Beard Foundation. His creativity and business acumen have made him one of Hawai'i's most celebrated and respected chefs. He still owns the six Roy's restaurants in Hawai'i, while the more than two dozen elsewhere are run by the Outback Steakhouse group. There are also outposts in Japan and Guam. Yamaguchi is always on the go, visiting restaurants, but he can occasionally be seen on the cooking line when he's in town and he personally appears at any number of charity events in Honolulu.

Sansei Seafood Restaurant and Sushi Bar

Waikīkī Beach Marriott Resort & Spa

2552 Kalākaua Ave.

931-6286

Dinner daily 5:30-10 p.m.; Fri., Sat. late-night 50 percent
    special, 10 p.m.-2 a.m.

Dave "D. K." Kodama loves to graze on a variety of dishes, and sushi is among his favorites. So when he returned to Hawai'i from several years of cooking on the mainland, where he learned European techniques, he opened up a sushi bar on Maui. Not a traditional sushi bar but the "creative" variety, with different ingredients, flavors and presentations.

Kodama expanded to Honolulu, where local folks loved his sometimes spicy and always delicious concoctions. Try the foie gras sushi, the mango and crab salad hand roll or a Sansei special roll with spicy crab and sweet Thai chili sauce. The menu includes nonsushi items, too, like Asian rock shrimp cakes and Japanese calamari salad, so you can dine just like the chef wants you to. This is a fun place to dine family style, sharing flavors and textures while sipping a cold beer or a well-paired wine.

EVERYDAY FARE

Fine dining isn't everyday dining. Sometimes you just want a good burger, a salad or a pizza. Here are some of the places that stand out in Honolulu, from ethnic holes-in-the-wall to simple cafes that are committed to fresh ingredients and good food. There are dozens and dozens more that are very good, to be sure. But these are the tried and true places that have contributed to the vibrant food scene in Honolulu and meet our standard of tasty food.

Andy's Sandwiches and Smoothies
2904 E. Mānoa Rd.
988-6161
Sun. 7 a.m.-2:30 p.m.; Mon.-Thurs. 7 a.m.-5:30 p.m.; Fri. 7 a.m.-
    4 p.m.; closed Sat.
Street parking

A tiny spot with a minimum of seats, Andy's has a loyal following in search of tasty, healthy food, vegetarian and non. We especially like the roast turkey sandwiches, made with real roast turkey.

Sandwiches piled high with sprouts and veggies, vegetarian burritos, breakfast omelets cooked to order, great pancakes, fruit smoothies—all the foods you want, made in a straightforward, healthy way.

Antonio's

4210 Wai'alae Ave.
737-3333
Tues.-Sat. 11:30 a.m.-8:30 p.m., Sun. noon-7:30 p.m.; closed
   Mon.
Parking available

At this New York–style pizzeria, the pizza has a crisp thin crust with the requisite cornmeal edge, tasty tomato sauce but not too much, sufficient but not overly done cheese and good toppings. Joe Tramontano and Anthony Romano know how to do it right. Philly cheese steaks, hoagies, salads and pasta dishes are all on the menu; eat them on the premises, hot and fresh from the oven, or

take them home. And be sure to have Neva Romano's New York–style cheesecake.

BluWater Grill
Hawai'i Kai Shopping Center
377 Keāhole St.
395-6224
Mon.-Thurs. 11 a.m.-11 p.m.; Fri., Sat. 11 a.m.-midnight; Sun.
    2:30-11 p.m.
Sunday brunch 10 a.m.-2:30 p.m.

This is one of the few places in Honolulu where you can dine at water's edge, where relaxation quickly sets the tone for the meal. Add fresh, distinctive food, creative drinks and a place where camaraderie reigns and you have a delightful neighborhood bistro. Tanya Phillips and chef Bill Bruhl are the owners, setting the standard for good service and food. Try the crispy fried moi with ginger and garlic; top it off with *liliko'i* crème brûlée. Sunday brunch is terrific, especially the free pancakes.

C&C Pasta
3605 Wai'alae Ave.
732-5999
Sun., Tues., Wed., Thurs. 5-9 p.m.; Fri., Sat. 5-10 p.m.; closed
    Mon.
Municipal parking lot and street parking

Proprietor Carla Magziar is Australian, but Italian at heart, and she opened this little cafe in Kaimukī with the intention of selling fresh homemade pastas and sauces and Italian foods for the consumer to take home and cook. Well, it turned into a restaurant that features rustic Italian dishes crafted by Magziar and her staff.

You can still get freshly made pasta by the sheet or cut into fettucine and linguine, and house-made sauces and sausages and other items to take home and turn into your own dishes. But most folks come here to dine at this BYOB restaurant.

Cafe Laufer

3565 Wai'alae Ave.
735-7717
Sun., Mon., Wed., Thurs. 10 a.m.-9 p.m.; Fri., Sat. 10 a.m.-10
    p.m.; closed Tues.
Municipal parking lot and street parking

A comfortable neighborhood cafe where you can get a hearty bowl of soup, sandwiches, salads, simple meals and delicious European-style pastries, all prepared on-site by owner Cyrus Goo. Nothing pretentious here, just good basic food.

✕ The Contemporary Café
2411 Makiki Heights Dr.
523-3362
Lunch Tues.-Sat. from 11:30 a.m., last order at 2 p.m.; Sun.
    noon-2 p.m.; closed Mon.
Parking available

This cafe, set amidst the lush grounds of an art museum, is a love-ly retreat just a few minutes away from the hustle and bustle of Honolulu below. Dine on simple and delicious fare here—food with a California touch, made with fresh local ingredients that shine. Chef Adam Gilbert does a fine job at this relaxing lunch venue.

D. K. Steakhouse
Waikīkī Beach Marriott Resort & Spa
2552 Kalākaua Ave.
931-6280
Dinner daily 5:30-10 p.m.
Parking in hotel

If you're looking for a big, thick, juicy steak, you can always go to Morton's or Ruth's Chris, two national chains that are popular in Honolulu. Or you can go to D. K. Steakhouse, run by D. K. Kodama of Sansei Seafood and Sushi fame. Kodama learned the ins and outs of butchering and dry aging beef and puts forth some terrific steaks along with the requisite sides of potatoes, rice and vegetables. Try the 22-ounce bone-in dry-aged rib eye steak—a tantalizing plateful of perfectly grilled, juicy beef. It doesn't get much better anywhere else.

El Burrito

550 Pi'ikoi St.

596-8225

Mon.-Thurs. 11 a.m.-8 p.m.; Fri., Sat. 11 a.m.-9 p.m.; closed
    Sun.

A hole-in-the-wall spot with 28 seats, this little eatery serves up well-seasoned, hearty and simple Mexican fare. Mario and Jolanda Manrique, originally from Mexico City, have been cooking up their well-known chimichangas and chicken Bethany for 20 years. Order the taco *al pastor*—a spicy pork taco—and you'll be delighted. Bring your own beer (or other spirits) to wash down the chips, guacamole and other tasty Mexican fare.

Formaggio

Market City Shopping Center

2919 Kapi'olani Blvd.

739-7719

Mon.-Thurs. 5 p.m.-midnight; Fri., Sat. 5 p.m.-2 a.m.; closed
Sun.

Parking available

Honolulu's first wine bar, Formaggio is an outgrowth of Fujioka's
wine store next door. Former wine salesman Wes Zane has taken
over this comfortable spot that serves up cheese plates, pizzas,
panini and salads that are above the ordinary. Short ribs and
heartier fare, too. Come here to eat, but mostly to sip and taste
wines, of which there is a fine selection. Live entertainment, too.

Golden Duck

1221 S. King St.
597-8088
Daily 10:30 a.m. to 11 p.m.
Parking in rear and on the street

The Golden Duck has been around for almost three decades, originally on McCully St. But it moved to this location a dozen years ago, and Aaron Fong took over the ownership in 2001. Wisely, he kept the same workers, and the food is as good as ever. We're talking local-style Chinese food, dishes like boneless minute chicken cake noodle, *kau yuk,* spareribs, salt and pepper shrimp, and *hum hee* chicken fried rice. The food here is the country-style food that Hawai'i's early Chinese immigrants cooked; it's comforting and tasty food.

Hale Vietnam

1140 12th Ave.
735-7581
Daily 10 a.m.-10 p.m.
Municipal parking lot and street parking

A casual neighborhood restaurant that happens to serve up some pretty good Vietnamese food at reasonable prices. Bowls of *phô* are well seasoned and served steaming hot; rice noodle dishes are always appointed with fresh herbs and vegetables; curries and other specialties are served up with friendly service. This is a good neighborhood spot with consistent food and service.

Hee Hing

449 Kapahulu Ave.
735-5544
Daily 10:30 a.m.-9 p.m.
Complimentary valet parking; street parking

Classic Cantonese Chinese food cooked up by the Lee family: lemon chicken, boneless minute chicken cake noodle, taro basket with tofu and vegetables, and roasted garlic pepper Dungeness crab are just some of the many dishes people have loved for over 40 years. Dim sum is served too; be sure to try the golden-fried shrimp pouch. For family dining or celebration banquets, Hee Hing is a good choice.

Imanas-Tei

2626 S. King St.
941-2626
Mon.-Sat. 5 -11:30 p.m.; closed Sun.
Limited parking; street parking

You'll have to hunt for this tucked-away restaurant, but once you get inside, you'll be impressed by the sophisticated ambiance created by the bamboo ceiling, light woods and effective lighting. The food is just as remarkable: sashimi, sushi, *shabu-shabu* and *nabe-mono* preparations like *chanko nabe*, the dish sumo wrestlers love. Keisuke "Casey" Asai also serves up traditional *izakaya* fare, small plates to whet and indulge the appetite while you're sipping sake or beer. We like this cozy, vibrant dining scene and well-prepared food.

India Cafe

Kilohana Square
1016 Kapahulu Ave.
737-4600
www.indiacafehawaii.com
Dinner 5-9 p.m. daily; until 9:30 on Fri. and Sat.
Lunch 11 a.m.-2:30 p.m., Fri. Sat. and Sun.
Parking available

Dosai, thin bread fashioned of fermented ground rice and lentils, is the specialty at this South Indian eatery run by Raja and Jiva Segaran, a father-son duo. Enjoy the *dosai* alongside fiery curries (they are not afraid to spice it up!) of lamb, chicken, shrimp or vegetables or have them with butter or coconut or sprinkled with sugar. While the focus here is on South India, you'll find samosas, naan and *lassi* among the many menu offerings. The family lived in Malaysia, so Malaysian influences crop up too. Try the *thali*, the Indian "plate lunch" of various dishes served on a tray.

Jimbo's

1936 S. King St. #103
947-2211
Lunch Sun.-Thurs. 11 a.m.-2:45 p.m., Fri., Sat. 11 a.m.-2:45 p.m.
Dinner Sun.-Thurs. 5-9:45 p.m.; Fri. Sat. 5-10:30 p.m.

If you're an udon fan, you'll love the freshly made noodles in delicate broth served with a variety of toppings. Or have your udon stir-fried with a combination of meats and vegetables. Of course, there's nothing like owner Jimbo Motojima's *nabeaki* udon, served in a ceramic pot with mushrooms, vegetables, egg and tempura. If you don't like udon, go anyway for one of the delicious *donburi* dishes.

Kim Chee II

3569 Wai'alae Ave.
737-7733
Daily 10:30 a.m.-9 p.m.
Municipal parking lot and street parking

Many of today's Korean restaurants appeal to the sweet palates of local folks. But old-timers (descendants of the first wave of Korean immigrants to Hawai'i) are used to more savory seasonings. That's what Henry and Rose Chun have been cooking up since 1977: *kal bi, pul ko gi*, meat *juhn* and other Korean staples that are delicious and not too sweet. They are also known for their generous servings and moderate prices. Not a fancy place, but known for its good food and prompt service.

Kua Aina Sandwich Shop

Ward Village Shops
1116 'Auahi St.
591-9133
Mon.-Sat. 10:30 a.m.-9 p.m.; Sun. 10:30 a.m.-8 p.m.
Parking available

When you're in the mood for a good burger or any other kind of sandwich, this is the place to go. The Nebraska beef burger on a kaiser roll is the forte here, but try a mahimahi with Ortega chili, grilled 'ahi, roast turkey, BLT or pastrami sandwich and you'll be satisfied. Owner Terry Thompson has kept the grill sizzling at this location and at the flagship location in Hale'iwa on the North Shore for more than 30 years.

Mekong
1295 S. Beretania St.
591-8841
Lunch Mon.-Fri. 11 a.m.-2 p.m.
Dinner daily 5-9 p.m.
Parking next to florist; street parking

Since 1977 this small, unassuming restaurant has been serving some of the best Thai food in Honolulu. Consistently fresh and good food comes out of this kitchen: the crispy fish salad is excellent, as are the curries, stir-fried *ong choy* and sticky rice with mango. This is perhaps the first Thai restaurant in Honolulu, started by the Sananikone family that also runs Mekong II and Keo's restaurants and the Asian Grocery Store just a few doors away. We like the authenticity here and the modest but comfortable surroundings.

Murphy's Bar and Grill
2 Merchant St.
531-0422
Lunch Mon.-Fri. 11:30 a.m.-2:30 p.m.
Dinner daily 5-10 p.m.
Breakfast Sat. from 9:30 a.m.
Bar open daily 11 a.m.-2 a.m.
Street parking
gomurphys.com

One of Honolulu's oldest and finest drinking spots, holder of one of five original "Retail Spirit" licenses issued in the 1860s, Murphy's is just a wonderful place for good food. Owner Don Murphy's saloon caters to the lunchtime business crowd, the afterwork cocktail crowd and sports fans. Expect good sandwiches, salads, steaks and fish in no-nonsense preparations that have stood the test of time. It's the place to be on St. Patrick's Day in Honolulu and for all major sporting events.

Olive Tree Cafe
4614 Kīlauea Ave.
737-0303
Dinner daily 5-10 p.m.
Parking available; street parking

A very casual, indoor-outdoor cafe without waiters that serves up delicious Greek specialties. Order at the counter and wait for your name to be called. Start with tabbouleh, baba ghanoush, dolmas, or hummus; then have fish *souvlaki* with pita and *tzatziki*. Owner Savas Mojarrad cooks it all from scratch, fresh and tasty. BYOB at this popular and crowded spot.

Pavilion Cafe
Honolulu Academy of Arts
900 S. Beretania St.
532-8734
Lunch Tues.-Sat. from 11:30 a.m., last reservation at 1:30 p.m.
    Closed Mon.; open every third Sun.
Parking available; street parking

One of the best spots in all of Honolulu for lunch: chef Mike Niven's salads, sandwiches and entrées are always about the ingredients—fresh, embellished a little, but always naturally tasty. Try the *piadina*, a "sandwich" of prosciutto, mozzarella, tomatoes, cucumbers, pesto and arugula in a folded thin flatbread. Grilled Anaheim peppers with capers, anchovies and garlic demand that you soak up the olive oil they're cooked in. White bean salad is always a good choice. This is one of only a few places in Honolulu where you can get a good roast chicken. Always leave room for comforting desserts at this outdoor cafe that is one of Honolulu's gems.

Spices
2671 S. King St.
949-2679
Lunch Tues.-Fri. 11:30 a.m.-2 p.m.
Dinner Tues.-Sat. 5:30-10 p.m.; Sun. 5:30-9 p.m.
Closed Mon.
Street parking

Southeast Asian food is well executed in this small and visually rich restaurant. The flavors of Thailand, Vietnam, Burma, and Laos are represented here at the hand of Somphong "Pony" Norindr, originally from Laos and educated in France and Switzerland. He is an architect in addition to being a chef, so the fresh ingredients in rich and spicy sauces are beautifully presented, well seasoned and balanced. Try the Burmese-style egg noodles in curry broth and the exotic house-made ice creams of durian, pandan and lemongrass and chili. Though the place is casual, its food and ambiance give it an upscale feel.

Sushi Land
1610 S. King St.
945-2256
Mon.-Sat. 10 a.m.-10 p.m., last order 9:30 p.m.; closed Sun.
Parking available

The sushi here is unremarkable; good, but there are better places. What we like here is the 'Ahi Salad, an attractive bowlful of chopped iceberg lettuce, julienne of cucumbers and carrots, shredded cabbage, slivers of green onion and nori, a spoonful of *tobiko* and a generous topping of *'ahi* sashimi. Drizzle on some sesame seed or *ko chu jang* dressing or both, mix it all up and delight in the crunchy and soft textures and spicy flavor. The addition of warm rice makes it even better. And you'll feel as if you've just eaten a healthy meal—which you have.

Teddy's Bigger Burgers

134 Kapahulu Ave.
926-3444
Daily 10:30 a.m.-9 p.m.

7192 Kalaniana'ole Hwy.
808 394-9100
Daily 10:30 a.m.-9 p.m.

This is the reinvented 1950s burger joint of Rich Stula and Tedd Tsakiris, who set out to serve the best burger in town. They do it: 100 percent chuck burgers, no fillers added, hand shaped, grilled

and served with lettuce, onion, tomato, pickle and their special secret sauce. Get a five-ounce patty or one that's larger; top it with cheese or have it with house-made teriyaki sauce. French fries, of course, and thick, delicious milkshakes—just like the '50s.

Tokkuri-Tei

611 Kapahulu Ave. #102
739-2800
Lunch Mon.-Fri. 11 a.m.-2 p.m.
Dinner Mon.-Sat. 5:30 p.m. to midnight; closed Sun.

Izakaya have become a popular dining option in Honolulu: small plates of food to accompany a beer, sake or even wine. Hideaki "Santa" Miyoshi has established quite a reputation for some very innovative dishes using prime local ingredients in addition to traditional sushi and *izakaya* fare. He's taken a liking to *poke,* and spider *poke* is one of his signature dishes. We like the casualness of this tavern and the delicious food.

Town

3435 Wai'alae at 9th Ave.
735-5900
Pastries and coffee Mon.-Sat. from 6:30 a.m.
Lunch Mon-Sat. 11 a.m.-2 p.m.
Dinner Mon.-Sat. from 5:30 p.m., last order at 9:30 p.m., Fri.,
    Sat. last order at 10 p.m.
Closed Sun.

A new addition to the Honolulu dining scene, Town fills the niche for light, natural food that speaks for itself. Chef/owner Ed Kenney is creatively simple in his preparations, allowing his mostly organic pantry of ingredients from MA'O Organic Farm in Wai'anae to shine. Flatbreads topped with really ripe, tasty tomatoes and herbs or a white bean purée and cucumbers, *'ahi* tartare on top of risotto cakes, sumptuous salads, braised oxtails, grilled fish—all are well executed to let the naturalness of the food come through. Be sure to have the wonderful buttermilk *panna cotta* for dessert. The restaurant is hip and edgy, acoustically nightmarish, but certainly worthy of dining at because of its stellar food.

Vino
Restaurant Row
500 Ala Moana Blvd.
524-8466
Wed., Thurs. 5:30-9:30 p.m.; Fri. Sat. 5:30-10:30 p.m.
Looking for a light Italian-inspired bite and some great wines? This cozy wine bar will fill the cravings. Grilled asparagus topped with a sunny-side-up quail egg and truffle oil, deep-fried mozzarella with vine-ripened tomatoes, cheese platters and cured meats, pastas, too, all meant for nibbling while you sip from a long

list of wines, many Italian, many not. Master sommelier Chuck Furuya and a knowledgeable staff are on hand to guide your choices. Special tastings and events are always going on here, too.

Yanagi Sushi

762 Kapi'olani Blvd.

597-1525

Lunch daily 11 a.m.-2 p.m.

Dinner Mon.-Sat. 5:30 p.m.-2 a.m., last order at 1:30 a.m.; Sun. 5:30-10 p.m.

This Japanese restaurant and sushi bar buzzes with activity and is often sought out by visiting celebrities. Since 1978 Haruo Nakayama and his family have served up fresh sashimi and an excellent variety of sushi of ample portions at the 26-seat sushi bar. At the tables you can have *teishoku,* sukiyaki, *shabu-shabu* and an occasional Korean specialty. There's a 30-seat private dining room here too. Yanagi Sushi is one of Honolulu's top sushi bars for good reason.

Yu Chun Korean Restaurant
825 Ke'eaumoku St.
944-1994
Mon-Fri. 10 a.m.-10 p.m.; Sat. 11 a.m.-10 p.m.; closed Sun.

You'll find a varied menu of Korean food here, including house-made *mandoo, kal bi* and *duk kook*. But the reason people come here is for the "black noodles." It's really a dish called *naeng myun*, noodles in a cold seasoned broth, topped with vegetables. Here, the noodles happen to be black—a buckwheat and arrow-root noodle from Korea. The broth is beef-based, with lots of vegetables and seasonings, according to owner Myung Cha, who opened this small restaurant in 1997. Traditional *naeng myon* broth is usually doused with the liquid from kim chee, but Cha makes a sweeter broth here that is quite addictive. The spicy version with chili powder is even better; or order your black noodles warm with raw fish.

WHERE TO SHOP

SUPERMARKETS

Honolulu has four major supermarket chains: Foodland, Star, Times and Safeway. Foodland and Star are owned and operated by local families; Times and Safeway are mainland owned. Each one caters to its clientele, determined by the community in which it is situated. Foodland tries to be a bit more upscale, with specialty food products among its grocery selections, an in-house chef who prepares "gourmet food-to-go" in selected locations, La Brea and Grace Bakery breads from California and R. Field Wine stores-within-a-store at two locations, featuring fine wines, cheeses and imported specialty foods. All supermarkets have deli departments with food-to-go, much of which is brought in from the mainland, already prepared. Big-box retailers like Costco, Wal-Mart and Sam's Club also factor into the food-shopping scene as does Ranch 99, a mainland chain specializing in Asian food. Daiei is another local supermarket with an emphasis on Asian foods.

The important thing to remember is that about 75 percent of the "fresh" food in supermarkets is imported to Hawai'i from the mainland, primarily the U.S. West Coast, 2,400 miles away, and other countries. Most of our food arrives via container ships (perishable, seasonal fresh fruit and vegetables are sometimes air flown) that take a minimum of four days to make the journey from the West Coast. Add a day on either end for delivery to and from the dock and you have products that are almost a week old before they hit the supermarket shelves. Yes, that applies to milk, eggs, fruits, vegetables, meats, chicken and everything else that is labeled "fresh."

Beef is virtually all from the mainland, though you may find some pasture-raised North Shore Cattle Co. beef (see pages 110 and 163); lamb, chicken and veal (if you can ever find veal!) are all imported. You may run into the occasional display of island pork, but chances are it is a mainland pig slaughtered here and labeled as "island pork." Milk and eggs with an "Island Fresh" logo are fresh Hawai'i products.

Perhaps the best thing about shopping in our supermarkets is the fish department. You can count on fresh fish like 'ahi, mahimahi, marlin, swordfish, opah and other varieties caught by Hawai'i's trollers and longline fishermen (see pages 67–68). You'll also see a variety of shellfish and fish from everywhere else, usually "freshly" defrosted. Fresh-caught is so much better!

There is much in the way of locally grown fruits and vegetables at supermarkets, neighborhood grocery stores, Chinatown markets and farmers' markets. Consumers need to look for "island fresh" signs or ask for island-grown produce, which will be fresher than imports. Organic produce in supermarkets is mostly mainland grown, since there are few large-scale organic farmers in the state. Check natural food stores and farmers' markets for locally grown organic items.

If you are a discriminating shopper bent on finding fresh ingredients, food shopping can be a frustrating experience. You'll drive all over town to find the freshest and the best of local products. One store will have great tomatoes from a particular farmer; another will have a wider selection of locally grown greens. One store will have the cheese you're looking for; another will have a butcher who will cut you a thick pork chop. But food lovers on a hunt can manage to find what they're looking for, given the time, money and perseverance it takes.

FARMERS' MARKETS

The alternative to the supermarket for fresh produce is the farmers' market. There are dozens of them throughout Honolulu, featuring produce and flowers and catering to the food preferences of the communities they serve. But consumers should be aware of the distinctions among markets: some are true farmers' markets, with locally grown produce and farmers present; others are vendor markets, with imported and locally grown produce and some farmers present.

The Saturday Farmers' Market at Kapiʻolani Community College (KCC)
4303 Diamond Head Rd.
Sat. 7:30-11 a.m.
848-2074
Parking available
www.hfbf.org

In September 2003 Honolulu got a real farmers' market—real in the sense that farmers are present to sell their products and all of the products featured here are grown in the state of Hawaiʻi. No mainland produce is allowed here; that's a rule. What you'll find is the freshest of salad greens, herbs, Asian greens, papayas, pineapples, bananas, tomatoes, watercress, corn, beets, avocado and a whole lot more. You'll find boutique producers of lettuce, asparagus, hearts of palm, rambutan, mango, strawberries, lychee, persimmon, cherimoya, pomelo, Yukon Gold and red potatoes, heirloom tomatoes, sweet onions and just about anything else that grows in Hawaiʻi. What you won't find are items like garlic, carrots, storage onions, and russet potatoes, all mainland grown; island-grown broccoli and celery are sometimes available. You'll

find pasture-raised, hormone-free beef from North Shore Cattle Co. of Haleʻiwa. You can buy various cuts of beef or hamburger, or enjoy a burger or beef sausage in a bun, cooked on the spot.

Fresh fish is often available, as are a small crop of free-range eggs and the occasional chicken. Fresh tropical flowers are plentiful, as are orchid plants and potted culinary herbs and ornamentals.

And the best part: each Saturday morning a local chef takes over the breakfast booth and cooks up hot breakfast plates for market shoppers. There's Hawai'i-grown coffee, too, plain or made into cappuccinos and lattes; fried green tomatoes, fresh pastas and sauces, oatcakes, cookies, jams, jellies and sauces and a variety of prepared foods-to-go.

Talk about a social scene: this is the place to be on Saturday mornings for folks who live in the Kaimukī-Kāhala-Wai'alae area, though folks travel from other communities to join the fun. Buying locally grown produce is more than just a shopping expedition for these discriminating shoppers.

The Hawai'i Farm Bureau Federation sponsors this market and also operates two other markets on O'ahu:

The Kailua Thursday Night Farmers' Market, Thursday, 5 to 7:30 p.m., Kailua Town Center Parking Garage off Kailua Rd.

The Mililani Farmers' Market, Sundays 8 a.m. to noon, Mililani High School, 95-1200 Meheula Parkway, Mililani.

People's Open Markets
522-7088
27 locations each week on O'ahu

These markets were started in the 1970s by the City and County of Honolulu as a lower-priced alternative to supermarket shopping. They set up at more than two dozen locations on O'ahu each week; each market is in a neighborhood for about an hour, traveling to two or three locations in a day. Farmers and vendors must adhere to a price ceiling on products, so produce is generally 30 percent cheaper than at supermarkets. Some of the produce, sold by vendors, is the same produce you'd find in a supermarket or produce bought from big-box retailers, repacked and offered for sale. There are farmers, to be sure, often those with papayas, bananas, ethnic vegetables, flowers and aquaculture products grown on a small scale. Some of these products are wonderful, but you do have to search them out and ask if they are truly home-grown. Among the best of the City's markets

Kaumuali'i St., 700 Kalihi St., Sat., 8:15-9:30 a.m., where a mostly Filipino clientele gathers to shop for ethnic specialties.

Hawai'i Kai Park-n-Ride, 300 Keāhole St., Sat., 1-2 p.m.

Ward Farmers' Market
1020 'Auahi St.
Mon.-Sat. 7 a.m.-5 p.m.; Sun. 7 a.m.-1 p.m.
Parking available

Ward Farmers' Market is not really a farmers' market but a collection of food stores and stalls that specialize in Hawaiian foods, local snacks, fresh seafood and produce.

Haili's Hawaiian Food is one of the best places to buy a full array of Hawaiian foods. Take home some *kālua* pork, poi, *lomi* salmon and *pipikaula* for a feast. Haili's is also a caterer, supplying many a *lū'au* with all the authentic foods fit for a celebration. 808 593-8019. (See section on Hawaiian Food.)

Tropic Fish and Vegetables (591-2963) has been at the Ward Farmers' Market complex since it was established in 1951, selling fresh vegetables and fruits, most of them from local farmers and groceries, and lots of fresh island fish and *poke*. The Tanoue family runs the store in addition to its wholesale operation, which supplies fresh island fish to island restaurants, supermarkets and hotels and exports to mainland and Japan destinations. Next door is Tropic Diner, a popular hangout for island-style foods and *pau hana*–time cocktails and *pūpū*.

Jan Lin says she has the best crack seed selection in Honolulu: no doubt it's a good-sized selection, in addition to the

dried fish and seafood products that local folks like to snack on. But mostly, Lin's Market (593-8611) is known for its boiled peanuts (see page 49), sold by the pound. Lin's also stocks marlin jerky made on the island of Hawai'i.

If you're bargain hunting for chicken, visit Stanley's Chicken Market (593-9989). This chicken wholesaler/distributor counts at least 50 Chinese restaurants as customers and sells to the public at about 25 percent less than supermarket retail pricing. And if you get to know Dennis Kinoshita, the third-generation operator of Stanley's, he might even lower the price for you. All the chickens and eggs sold here are "fresh chilled" from the mainland (there are no commercial-scale chicken farmers left on O'ahu); chicken bones and feet are always available for making soup and other delicacies.

Marukai Market Place

593-9888
Mon.-Sat. 7 a.m.-8 p.m.; Sun. 7 a.m.-6 p.m.

Marukai Market Place is a Japanese food store at the 'ewa end of Ward Farmers' Market. The great thing about Marukai is the selection of all food things Japanese, mostly imported from Japan. Pickles, seasonings, sauces, snacks, sake, soy sauces, vinegars, noodles and frozen foods, plus prepared foods, *bentos*, fresh produce, fish and seafood are part of the selection.

If you're a discriminating rice eater, you'll want to shop here, where rice varieties are abundant. We're talking premium California-grown Japanese varieties and brands like Kohishikari, Akita Komachi, Tamanishiki, Haigamai and others. These premium-quality rice varieties have subtle differences to be sure, but once you've eaten them, plain old Calrose will never be the same. Soy sauces, too, come in a wide range of brands and styles, as do rice vinegars, miso and sake. Since most of the grocery items are imported from Japan, labels are in Japanese. Ask the staff if you need help finding what you need.

Convenience is also important: American food products and a limited selection of Filipino, Chinese and Korean foods are available too. And don't overlook the many Hawai'i-produced food products.

Shopping in this compact store is like exploring the basement food area of a Japanese department store. The company originated in Osaka, Japan, as an exporter of Japanese food and lifestyle products to Hawai'i and Los Angeles. Marukai Wholesale Mart was established in 1987 at 2310 Kamehameha Hwy. (808 845-5051), offering discounted prices on food and home furnishings to its member shoppers. A $10 membership gets you in for a year to select from its inventory of over 20,000 items. Marukai Market Place at Ward was opened in 2002 and will encompass 12,000 square feet of product by early 2006.

ETHNIC AND SPECIALTY STORES

Asian Grocery Store
1319 S. Beretania St.
593-8440
Mon.-Sat. 9 a.m.-5:30 p.m.
Street parking

When Southeast Asian immigrants began coming to Hawai'i in 1975, the demand for ingredients of their homeland grew. The Sananikone family, who emigrated from Laos, got into the food business in 1976, establishing restaurants (Mekong 1 and 2, Keo's and Keoni's) and importing, distributing, wholesaling and retailing Asian food products.

The compact Asian Grocery Store stocks all the essentials for cooking Thai, Vietnamese, Chinese, Indonesian, Malaysian, Filipino and Indian foods. Bottled, canned and packaged items as well as fresh and frozen ingredients are available here plus some cooking and serving implements for that authentic meal. Best of all you can come with your recipe or cookbook in hand, find the ingredients and then get some cooking advice from the knowledgeable staff. Even if you're not going to cook something, you can get lots of information as you peruse the wide assortment of products.

Gourmet Foods Hawaii
740 Kopke St.
841-8071
Mon.-Fri. 7 a.m.-3 p.m.
Parking available

If you're a caterer or just a home cook who throws big parties, you'll be intrigued to find this out-of-the-way food supplier. What you'll find here are prepared foods, ready to cook and serve, like coconut-coated shrimp ready for the deep fryer, skewered chicken and beef, filo hors d'oeuvres, sausages, foie gras and other pates. Want to make guava jam or passion fruit curd? You'll find pure frozen purée in gallon-size jugs. Because this company sells to hotels, restaurants and airline caterers, you can expect good quality and fair pricing. You have to buy in bulk, so plan on a big gathering of friends.

Hans Weiler Foods

1329 Mo'onui St.
847-2210
Mon.-Fri. 7:30-4:30 p.m.; Sat. 9 a.m.-1 p.m.
Limited parking

Looking for blocks of chocolate by the pound, meringue powder, premade pastry crusts, fruit syrups, fillable chocolate cups, food coloring, cake decorations and other pastry and baking supplies? Domestic and imported items are in the inventory of this supplier to restaurants and bakeries that happily services home bakers. Peruse the excellent selection of professional bakeware and patisserie and confectionary paraphernalia. You can even get a monogrammed chef's outfit and professional books.

India Market

2570 S. Beretania St. #105
946-2020
Daily 10 a.m. to 8 p.m.
Parking available

"Indian, Middle Eastern and South Pacific groceries" reads the sign in front of this small grocery store just 'Ewa of University Avenue. Mohammed and Rehnuma Khan are the proprietors, both originally from Fiji but well versed in the foods of the countries they represent in their store. There's kava from Fiji, but most grocery items, frozen foods and refrigerated items are for Indian and Middle Eastern cuisine. Basmati rice, lentils of all colors, spices, pickles and chutney, naan, ready-to-eat curry packs, Shan seasoning mixes, *paneer*, feta, tea and coffee are neatly arranged and organized in this compact space. And just in case you're looking for some Vegemite, you'll find it here, too, amidst DVDs, videos and other items. Browsing this fascinating store will make you hungry.

Island Epicure at Y. Hata & Co.

285 Sand Island Access Road
447-4100
Mon.-Fri. 7:30 a.m.-4 p.m., Sat. 7:30 a.m.-noon
Parking available

Y. Hata & Co. is a major food wholesaler/distributor in Hawai'i, supplying hotels, restaurants, the military, schools and institutions with chilled and frozen foods, canned items, baking supplies, dietary foods, beverages, equipment and a host of other items. Under its roof is Island Epicure, a wholesale/retail store that sells gourmet food items like olive oil, vinegar, mustards, pastas, sauces, salad dressings and other canned, bottled and packaged specialty food items. These are the items top chefs—and other food lovers, too—like to include in their repertoire of ingredients for today's contemporary and upscale plates. At Island Epicure you can also find things like foie gras, cheeses, pates and other gastronomic delights. Prices here are good, but keep an eye out for dates on perishable items. You may also have to buy a larger quantity that you want.

It's Chili in Hawaii

2080 S. King St.
945-7070
Tues.-Sat. 10 a.m.-6 p.m.; Sun. 10:30 a.m.-3 p.m.
Parking available

This is a store for chili heads. Chili sauces, salsas, jellies and all things chili are stocked here, including Hatch, New Mexico green chilis. The largest selection of chili sauces in one place in Honolulu can be found and sampled here; on Saturdays, green chili stew is available. Owner Gary Toyama keeps frozen tamales stocked too; this 11-year-old Honolulu institution is always onto chili trends.

Mazal's Kosherland

555 N. King St. #113 (Kingsgate Plaza)
848-1700
Sun.-Thurs. 12 a.m.-7 p.m.; Fri. 10 a.m.-3 p.m.; closed Sat. and
    Jewish holidays
Parking available
www.kosherland.com

A small store with a devout following, Mazal's is Honolulu's only kosher food store, supplying the small Jewish community with a wider variety of traditional foods than found in supermarkets. You'll find a full line of groceries from Israel, as well as cheeses, yogurts, breads, cold cuts, chicken, Osem's meals on the go, gefilte fish, Israeli salads, canned goods, cookies, cakes and snacks.

The store was opened just a couple of years ago by Ifat Sharabi and named for her grandmother. The store is under the supervision of Chabad of Hawaii, a Jewish orthodox organization. Sharabi also has prepared foods to go and offers Shabbat meals, especially nice for visitors observing Jewish food rituals.

Mercado de la Raza

1315 S. Beretania St.
593-2226
Mon.-Fri. 9:30 a.m.-6:30 p.m., Sat. 10 a.m.-6:30 p.m.; Sun.
    noon-5 p.m.
Street parking

Martha Minn is the proprietor of this small but well-stocked Latin grocery frequented by Honolulu's growing community of Latinos from Mexico, Central and South America and the Caribbean. Dried chilis to make enchilada sauce, Mexican white cheese, beverages, teas, canned and bottled sauces and condiments, tortillas and some cooking equipment can all be found here.

Minn also makes some pretty mean fresh salsas and guacamole. Tamales, six different kinds, are made twice a month (the second and last Saturdays of the month) and are especially abundant during the Christmas holiday season. She keeps her store well stocked with the essentials of Latin cuisines in general and even gets a few farmers to grow habanero chilis, *epazote* and a few other delicacies. Since 1994, Minn has been an important part of the Honolulu food scene and a font of information on South of the Border cooking.

Palama Super Market

1210 Dillingham Blvd.
847-4427
Mon.-Sat. 8:30 a.m.-8:30 p.m.; Sun. 9 a.m.-8:30 p.m.
Parking available

1670 Makaloa St. near Kalākaua
945-3900
Daily 9 a.m.-9 p.m.
www.palamamarket.com

All foods and other things Korean can be found at Honolulu's two Korean markets: Palama Market (two locations) and Queen's Super Market. We prefer shopping at Palama, where displays seem more organized, produce fresher and items more plentiful.

At Palama, you'll be amazed at all the different varieties of kim chee; side dishes of *taegu*, bracken fern, fish and other pickled items. Shopping here is like shopping at a natural foods store: you'll find ancient grains like millet, sorghum and barley; beans of all colors, shapes and sizes; and unique items like pumpkin and black rice flour. Dried vegetables like zucchini and eggplant, ground chili pepper, seaweed of all shapes and sizes, and noodles galore are part of the wide selection. In the meat section you'll find thinly sliced beef for making *pul ko gi and* short ribs for *kal bi,* as well as pork and fish. In the freezer case you'll find fish, seafood of all kinds, *mandoo*, noodles, *duk* and a whole lot more. And of course there's fresh produce, especially Korean radish and *won bok* for kim chee making.

Palama Super Market also manages to squeeze in some appliances, housewares and tabletop items, cosmetics, videos and other imported Korean consumer goods. There's always freshly made *duk* of all shapes and sizes for savory and sweet eating as well as Korean plates and other foods to go. And you can't leave without some *keem pahb*, a Korean seaweed and rice roll with meat, vegetables and pickles, brushed with sesame oil, that makes for a fine meal.

R. Field Wine Company

Foodland Beretania
1460 S. Beretania St.
596-9463
Daily 10 a.m.-8 p.m.
Parking available

In Honolulu, this is it for gourmet food stores. Small, tucked within a supermarket and severely limited in its selection for lack of space, R. Field Wine Company does the best that it can under the circumstances. This epicurean shop began as a wine store and continues to feature some very fine wine selections, although they are usually priced higher than at other wine stores around town.

It can be pricey to buy a pound of San Daniele prosciutto or an ounce of caviar. But it's unlikely you'll find it anywhere else. There's a small but good selection of cheeses, catering to local tastes; deli meats, sausages and salami, smoked duck breast, smoked salmon, assorted pates, foie gras, caviar; fresh herbs and greens from Nalo Farms; and other specialty produce from mainland farms. Products from D'Artagnan and Trois Petit Cochons can be found here; Valrhona and Neuhaus chocolates, too. Pastas, bottled sauces, olives, olive oils, vinegars, capers, preserves and all those other bottled, canned and packaged foods that make up great food stores are here, just limited in variety and depth. But you can usually find the item you need for most of today's cooking.

A small but selective inventory of wines competes for space with the specialty foods but you'll find cutting-edge wines from small-domain producers that handcraft their wines. Richard Field has departed the shop he founded that is now part of the Foodland chain, but his able staff continues to select fine vintages along with spirits and cigars for a usually more affluent clientele.

The folks at R. Field are friendly and knowledgeable, especially about wines. If they're not busy slicing salami, they are a great bunch to chat with about what's happening on the food scene. There's always something to taste here, too, and no doubt food lovers will find something interesting to buy. There's another location at Foodland in Kailua.

Shirokiya

Ala Moana Center, mall level near Macy's
973-9111
Mon.-Sat. 9:30 a.m.-9 p.m.; Sun. 9:30 a.m.-7 p.m.

Shirokiya started business in Hawai'i in 1959, a branch of one of Tokyo's oldest department stores, founded in 1662. The department store here is now locally owned and continues to stock a wide variety of consumer goods and lots of good food, mimicking department stores in Japan, albeit on a smaller scale. You can find seasonings, snacks, frozen foods, seafood and general grocery items here. But the best thing is the *bentos*, boxed meals of assorted foods to take home or eat in the small seating area, prepared fresh and always tasty. Japanese regional food specialties are often promoted at Shirokiya, featuring a special noodle dish, *mochi* or sushi; it's a great opportunity to taste a bit of Japan in Honolulu. St. Germain Bakery is housed within Shirokiya, so be sure to grab a crisp French baguette while you're shopping.

Yamasin Market

1475 N. King St.
808 841-0808
Mon.-Sat. 10 a.m.-9 p.m.
Parking available

Peter Woo opened this market over 15 years ago because he lived among folks from the South Pacific. He supplies them with the foods of home: canned corned beef, canned mackerel, taro from Fiji, bananas, taro leaves and home-cooked dishes in a buffet warmer. There are frozen meats and poultry, too. This is a small market where sizes are big but variety is limited, but Polynesians and Micronesians find plenty to buy here.

NATURAL/HEALTH FOODS MARKETS

Down to Earth

2525 S. King St.
947-7678
Daily 7:30 a.m.-10 p.m.
Parking in building and on street

While it isn't large by any stretch of the imagination, Down to Earth is Honolulu's largest natural foods market. It is a vegetarian market: no animal products here, including eggs, but the store does stock dairy items.

You'll find a wide range of products, many with upscale labels (Wolfgang Puck organic soups, for instance), for the health-conscious consumer and cook. An excellent assortment of grains, beans, cereals, rice, dried fruits, nuts and seeds, is offered in bulk so you can buy what you need. Fresh-baked breads, snack foods, beverages, cheeses, and canned and bottled items, as well as fresh produce, much of which is mainland organic, all fit into this compact store that also stocks nutritional supplements and lifestyle products. Oh yes, there's a deli too, with an assortment of foods-to-go.

The company started on Maui in 1977 and has five locations, three on Oʻahu and two on Maui, making it one of the largest natural food chains in the United States.

Huckleberry Farms

1613 Nuʻuanu Ave.
524-7960
Mon.-Sat. 9 a.m.-8 p.m., Sun. 9 a.m.-6 p.m.
Parking available

Pete Pascua started this natural foods store and its nutritional supplement store a few doors away. Besides the general assortment of mostly organic and and mainland produce and general grocery items, Huckleberry features a wide array of frozen meat products: Shelton Farm chickens, organic beef, pork, turkey and lamb from Harmony Farms, buffalo and ostrich. Bulk grains, nuts, spices, cereals and snacks are offered here, as well as a small selection of deli-made soups, sandwiches and salads that you can grab and go. Selections are limited, but turnover is high at this neighborhood market.

Kokua Market

2643 S. King St.
941-1922
Daily 8:30 a.m.-8:30 p.m.
Parking available in back

This natural foods co-op has been in Honolulu for more than three decades, featuring a limited but good assortment of natural foods, including animal products. If you're on the hunt for Rocky free-range or Rosie antibiotic-free chickens, Big Island Poultry Vegefed eggs, Diestel turkey and pasture-raised Hawai'i-grown Kulana beef, you'll find them here.

Kokua offers its shoppers more locally grown and produced foods than the other natural foods markets in Honolulu. La Gelateria gelatos and sorbets, for example, can be found in the freezer case; produce from island organic farmers, seasonal fruit from backyard farmers, organic Kona coffee and other items produced locally are in the mix. Grains, beans, spices and other pantry staples are offered in bulk.

You can join the co-op as a member/owner for a refundable fee; member specials are offered, and a rebate is in the planning stages. Otherwise, just walk in and shop and enjoy the small deli that offers takeout foods.

'Umeke Market Natural Foods and Deli

4400 Kalaniana'ole Hwy.
739-2990
Mon.-Sat. 8 a.m.-8 p.m.; Sun. 9 a.m.-8 p.m.
www.umekemarket.com

'Umeke is the Hawaiian word for calabash, usually a carved wooden bowl once used in cooking and transporting food. As suggested by its name, this market, run by the Yamaguchi family, who have been in the grocery business for generations, is a calabash of good wholesome products.

What you'll find in this bright and cheery locale is a nice assortment of food products: fresh produce from local and mainland organic farmers; Kulana beef from the island of Hawai'i; Rocky (free-range) and Rosie (organic) chickens, Diestel turkey, bison, ostrich, elk, venison, Big Island Vegefed eggs, and grocery items chosen for their healthier aspects.

In the deli department, busy folks on the go can't get enough of the focaccia sandwiches, bison burgers, hummus, roasted free-range chickens and other ready-to-eat foods. This is the newest of Honolulu's natural food stores, just two years old, and by far the most pleasant for shopping.

BAKERIES

Hawai'i residents have a sweet tooth, and they like to indulge in sweet treats of all kinds. Bakery reputations are often based on a single item that appeals to the local palate: light, soft and airy textures, subtle flavors and sweet sweets. Ted's Bakery in Hale'iwa, for example, is known for its chocolate *haupia* pie, available in supermarkets. Lee's Bakery in Chinatown (see page 143) has a reputation for custard pie. Leonard's is the place to get hot malassadas (see page 40). Napoleon's Bakery at Zippy's is well known for its Napples. A number of Japanese-style French bakeries—Panya, Pelio, St. Germain—offer a different repertoire of sweet and savory delights with subtly sweet and light doughs. Bakeries in Honolulu are numerous and destinations in themselves.

Ba-Le Bakery

2242 Kamehameha Hwy.
847-4600
Daily 7 a.m.-7 p.m.
Parking available

Ba-Le Sandwich shops throughout Honolulu serve up terrific croissants and French baguettes that are all made here at the bake shop. But you'll find a lot more here—a full line of baked goods such as pastries, cakes, pies, breads, brownies, cookies and more. Expect European-style breads at the hands of chief baker Rodney Weddle as well as delicate and scrumptious desserts. Owner Thanh Lam caters to airlines, hotels and other food service companies. His bake shop is state of the art. Ba-Le also participates in Hawaii Farm Bureau Federation farmers' markets (see pages 109–111).

Dee Lite Bakery/St. Germain

1930 Dillingham Blvd.
847-5396
Daily 5 a.m.-9 p.m.

Ala Moana Center
1450 Ala Moana Blvd.
Street level near Foodland
955-6664
Mon.-Sat. 7 a.m.-9 p.m.; Sun. 8 a.m.-7 p.m.
Mall level in Shirokiya
955-1711
Mon.-Sat. 8 a.m.-9 p.m.; Sun. 9 a.m.-7 p.m.
Parking available

Three other locations in Honolulu

Herbert Matsuba started Dee Lite Bakery and created the spongy, tropical-fruit–flavored chiffon cakes for which it is famous.

Coconut, guava, and rainbow (guava, passion fruit and lime) are the flavors he incorporated into the spongy cakes and fillings that have made local folks swoon. Dee Lite was bought by St. Germain of America in 1990, adding its French breads and pastries to the lineup of baked goods.

Today Dee Lite cakes are still popular and true to the original recipe. They can be found in St. Germain locations. The St. Germain name, introduced at Shirokiya at Ala Moana Center in 1977, is recognized for its Japanese-style French baked goods. Perhaps the best thing about St. Germain is its crisp, crackly French baguettes, as close to Paris as you can get.

Liliha Bakery
515 N. Kuakini St.
531-1651
Daily except Mon., 24 hours a day
Parking available

The Takakuwa family has been running this bakery since the 1950s, offering a wide variety of pastries and desserts. Chantilly cake is a specialty; German chocolate and chocolate dobash cakes, too. But most of all it's the Coco Puffs that bring people here: a cream puff shell filled with chocolate pudding and topped with Chantilly icing. More than 3,000 of these signature buttery treats are made and sold each day, a testament to their local following.

More than just a place for delicious baked goods, Liliha Bakery is a homey neighborhood coffee shop with 18 seats at a counter serving up local comfort food without any frills but with friendly and efficient service. Light-as-a-feather pancakes for breakfast are a signature item; ask for a grilled butter roll, biscuit or cornbread. For lunch and dinner, there are burgers, beef stew and curry, saimin, meat loaf and other local favorites. When hunger strikes, go to Liliha Bakery, open 24 hours a day.

Patisserie

Kahala Mall Shopping Center
4211 Wai'alae Ave.
735-4402
Mon.-Sat. 7 a.m.-9 p.m.; Sun. 7 a.m.-5 p.m.
Parking available

Wyland Waikīkī Hotel
2200 Kūhiō Ave. at Royal Hawaiian Ave.
922-9752
Mon.-Sat. 6 a.m.-9 p.m.; Sun. 6 a.m.-8 p.m.
www.thepatisserie.com

Each of Honolulu's bakeries fills a niche, and Patisserie's European-style offerings are undoubtedly among the best. Hearty, chewy breads, delectable pastries and dreamy Chantilly and dobash cakes have had a following for nearly 40 years. Rolf's *lavosh*, a popular Armenian cracker bread in Hawai'i, is produced here and available in supermarkets and on the tables of many fine-dining establishments. The deli menu and dinner nights at the

Kahala Mall location reflect German specialties. Seasonally available Dresdner Stollen is wonderfully delicious; you can't go wrong with an apple fritter with coffee. Owners Robert and Colleen Paparelli have taken over from founder Rolf Winkler, keeping the recipes and traditions going. You can also order from the main bakery at 3210 Ualena St; 836-7900.

WINE, BEER AND SPIRITS SHOPS

Honolulu has become an international city when it comes to wine, beer and spirits. Sure, you may have to pay a bit more because of shipping costs, but better to have them at a higher price than not at all. While some wine aficionados may tout their private shipments, exploring the offerings of the shops listed here will reveal a wide variety of choices; supermarkets and big-box retailers offer everyday fare, too.

One thing to always keep in mind when you're buying wine is the weather: a hot day can ruin just-purchased wine sitting in the trunk of your car as you finish up your errands. Keep wines in air conditioning or in coolers and store them in cool corners of your home.

Fujioka's
2919 Kapiʻolani Blvd.
739-9463
Mon.-Sat. 10 a.m.-8 p.m., Sun. 11 a.m.-5 p.m.
Parking available

Lyle Fujioka opened this wine store in 1999 so Honolulu folks wouldn't have to drive to Haleʻiwa on the North Shore to buy his wine selections. He sold it in 2004 to Times Supermarkets and is now a consultant to the 12-store chain. Fujioka's maintains its stature among wine stores, featuring a wide selection of domestic and imported vintages, especially from Italy. There's a limited supply of specialty food items, a good selection of sakes and spirits and a knowledgeable staff to help you find what you want.

H. A. S. R. Wine Co. (see pages 142–143)

Liquor Collection
Ward Warehouse
1050 Ala Moana Blvd.
524-8808
Mon.-Sat. 10 a.m.-9:30 p.m.; Sun. 10 am.-6 p.m.
Parking available

Beer aficionados will find what they're looking for at this shop that is more than two decades old. Ming Koschi, the owner, keeps an inventory of over 150 beers and a fine collection of liquor. You'll find some wines in this old-fashioned liquor store, but beer and spirits are why you come here.

R. Field Wine Company (see page 120)

Tamura Fine Wine and Liquors
1216 10th Ave.
735-7100
Mon.-Sat. 9:30 a.m.-8 p.m.; Sun. 9:30 a.m.-7 p.m.
Parking available

Perhaps the broadest selection of wines can be found in this wine store with arguably the best prices in Honolulu. This is not a discount store; it is an unstuffy neighborhood store (folks come here for a bottle of wine to take to restaurants within the area) with a full range of wines from low-priced jugs to fine vintages. "Balance," "depth," "well crafted" and "good prices" are the operative terms here. Be sure to ask what's in the Back Room, where limited-supply trophy wines are stored, not all of which are high end. You can also stock up on cheese, *poke,* organic and specialty foods, and Riedel wine glasses, as well as microbrews and a full selection of spirits and other beverages.

Vintage Wine Cellar
1249 Wilder Ave.
523-9463
Daily 10 a.m.-7 p.m.
Parking available

This is Honolulu's oldest wine store, founded by Allen Kam and now in the capable hands of his son Jay Kam. There's a love of

wine in this family and long-established relationships with vintners, especially French vintners, reflected in the inventory of this
small and personable shop. Knowledgeable staff can help you
make wine selections; there's a limited selection of good beers,
and titanium stemware might catch your fancy.

The Wine Stop

1809 S. King St.
946-3707
Mon.-Thurs. 10 a.m.-9 p.m.; Fri., Sat. 10 a.m.-10 p.m.; Sun. 11
      a.m.-7 p.m.
Street parking
www.thewinestophawaii.com

"Eclectic" is the word often used to describe the wine selections of
this cozy wine shop. But "affordable" and "food friendly" might be
more appropriate—at least those are the qualities Kim Karalovich
and Liane Fu had in mind when they opened this shop in 2003.
This small store features boutique wineries as well as mainstream
ones, microbrews, sakes, fine spirits, wine accessories and gifts
and a very limited selection of cheeses, caviars and other food-
stuffs. Free Saturday afternoon wine tastings, a newsletter, a wine
club, and seminars are all part of this store's concept.

COOKWARE STORES

The Compleat Kitchen
Ala Moana Center
1450 Ala Moana Blvd.
944-1741
Mon.-Sat. 9:30 a.m.-9 p.m.; Sun. 10 a.m.-7 p.m.
Parking available

Kahala Mall
4211 Wai'alae Ave.
737-5827
Mon.-Sat. 10 a.m.-9 p.m.; Sun. 10 a.m.-5 p.m.
Parking available

Before Williams-Sonoma came to Hawai'i, there was The
Compleat Kitchen. Since 1976, this compact and well-stocked

shop of culinary wares for the kitchen has fulfilled the needs of Hawai'i's cooks and bakers, offering paraphernalia as well as cooking advice from the salespeople, who are often cooks and bakers themselves. Known for its wide selection of gadgets, the store stocks a basic array of cookware and bakeware, small electrical appliances, tabletop and decorative accessories for the kitchen and dining room and a well-selected array of imported, domestic and island food products. It's an adult toy store that makes you want to go home and cook.

The Executive Chef
Ward Warehouse
1050 Ala Moana Blvd.
596-2433
Mon.-Sat. 10 a.m.-9 p.m.; Sun. 10 a.m.-5 p.m.

This well-stocked cookware store has just about anything an executive chef, and home chefs too, could want. A wide selection of cookware, bakeware, gadgets, coffeemakers, storage containers and everything else for the kitchen (and bath) are stocked here in a generous space. A limited selection of specialty food products is stocked; the emphasis here is on the nuts and bolts of cooking and entertaining.

CHINATOWN

Chinatown, bordered by Beretania St. and Nimitz Hwy., River St. and Nu'uanu Ave., is a vibrant section of Honolulu abundant with ethnic flavors and adventures for the food lover. Chestnut brown roast ducks, caramel-colored chickens and red barbecued pork hang in street-side windows. Fresh papayas, bananas and pineapples are displayed in open-air bins. Asian greens are piled high. Noodlemakers bustle about in their flour-dusted shops. Pig carcasses are carried to a butcher's stall. The aroma of just-cooked *char siu* wafts in the air as a full pan passes you in the arms of the maker. Leimakers nimbly string fresh fragrant flowers into Hawai'i's welcoming garland.

Established around 1870, Chinatown was a magnet for Chinese immigrants who wanted to start their own businesses after their plantation contracts concluded. Watchmakers, jewelers, tailors, tinsmiths, laundrymen, bakers, shoemakers, grocers and food vendors established a community of stores. An influx of Filipinos made them the majority of the Chinatown population, but that has changed in the last 30 years as more recent immigrants from Vietnam, Laos and Hong Kong have settled here.

In 1896 a fire that was purposely set to rid the area of bubonic plague accidentally decimated a large area of Chinatown. The area was rebuilt and thrives today with a variety of mostly Chinese, Filipino and Southeast Asian businesses.

Chinatown is filled with grocery stores, herbalists and acupuncturists, jewelers, fabric and clothing shops, video stores, lei stands and restaurants all worthy of exploration. Maunakea Street is considered the main street of Chinatown. Parking in Chinatown can be somewhat challenging, but there are a number of municipal lots with reasonable parking rates. Everyone seems to be in Chinatown at midday: a good time to be there to experience the vibrancy of the area, though it can get crowded and difficult to maneuver the sidewalks. Most shops open around 7 a.m. and close by 3 p.m.

There are three "shopping centers" within Chinatown—Oahu Market, Kekaulike Market and Maunakea Marketplace—and dozens and dozens of shops in between.

Kekaulike Market
Kekaulike Mall, between King and Hotel Streets

This is an assemblage of vendors of various food items, including farm-raised fish, meats, kim chee and mostly fresh fruits and vegetables. The aisles are tight and quality and prices vary among vendors. The Cheap Market at one end generates a lot of activity: Sue Law and her family provide reasonably priced freshly grown vegetables from Kahuku, 'Ewa and Wai'anae farms. They have been selling produce for more than twenty years, obviously to a happy clientele.

Maunakea Marketplace
1120 Maunakea St.

Enter on Maunakea St. or Hotel St. into an area full of meat, chicken, seafood, fruits and vegetables. This Chinatown market-place seems to have a Filipino bent in its selection of produce items. Beyond the market area is a food court where you can dine on ethnic foods of all varieties: Filipino, Japanese, Chinese, Korean, Thai, Vietnamese. Be sure to try the *pad* Thai noodles at Malee, cooked to order and always good. Several Filipino stalls offer Visayan, Pangasinan and Ilocano styles of food. Outside the food area you can shop for Asian trinkets and souvenirs and people-watch in the courtyard.

Oahu Market
Corner of King and Kekaulike Streets

Oahu Market is a Chinatown institution that opened in the summer of 1904, established by Chinese entrepreneur Tuck Young. It became the major fish market of Honolulu, and today it still boasts several vendors offering fresh locally caught fish and *poke*. Nakashima Fish Market always has Kona crabs (see page 61) during the season, in addition to fish for sashimi. Ishimoto's has an assortment of bottom and reef fish and various kinds of *poke*.

Nakazato Fish Market and Hiro Fish Market stick mostly to 'ahi for sashimi.

Pork vendors are plentiful, including those who make *char siu* and Chinese-style roast pork, with its crispy skin. Kai Kee Meat Market is one of the many pork specialists here. Owner Yu Kai Long has been hacking up *char siu* and roast pork with his Chinese cleaver for almost twenty years, instantaneously cutting a pound of *char siu* into bite-size morsels on the round tree trunk cutting boards used by most Chinatown shops. You'll likely get a sample slice as Long wraps your purchase.

Signs for *povi masima* mean that corned beef, popular among South Pacific islanders, is available. If pig's head and blood, tripe, tongue or other offal is on your shopping list, you'll find it at Oahu Market (and other Chinatown butchers).

— CHINATOWN CULINARY TOUR —

Chinese Chamber of Commerce
42 N. King St.
808 533-3181
Mon. 9:30 a.m.
$10 per person

The Chinese Chamber of Commerce offers a walking tour of Chinatown focusing on the history and food culture of Hawai'i's Chinese community. Food lover and attorney Anthony Chang leads the tour, offering insights on regional specialties at various restaurants; history of the area, its buildings and street names; stops at various food shops, with samples; and tidbits on Chinese cuisine and techniques. Plan to spend at least three hours on this informative tour. No need to call ahead; just show up.

Find vegetables like wing beans, sweet potato leaves, skinny eggplant, bitter melon, lotus root, mountain yam and an assortment of fresh fruits, some exotic like jackfruit, rambutan and durian, among the many food stalls here. Ace Market always has a nice selection of produce.

There's no better place in Honolulu than Chinatown to get a fresh whole fish to steam in the traditional Chinese way. It's one of the best ways to eat fish; be sure to have plenty of rice alongside.

STEAMED FISH, CHINESE STYLE

3-pound whole fish or 4 6-ounce filets (or 4 whole 1-pound
    moi)
2 tablespoons fresh ginger, peeled and cut into fine juli-
    enne
1/2 cup peanut oil
1/3 cup soy sauce
4 green onions, cut into julienne
1/2 cup cilantro

If using whole fish, clean and scale. Make 3 to 4 incisions into sides of fish. Insert slivers of ginger into cavity and sprinkle over the top. If using fish filets, place ginger on top of fish. Place fish on steaming rack and steam, allowing 8 to 9 minutes per inch of thickness.

While fish is steaming, heat oil in a small saucepan until smoking. When fish is cooked, place on serving platter. Pour soy sauce over fish and top with green onions. Pour oil over fish, top with cilantro leaves and serve immediately. Serves 4.

CHINATOWN SHOPS OF INTEREST

Bo Wah Trading Co.
1037 Maunakea St.
537-2017
Mon.-Sat. 8 a.m.-6 p.m.; Sun. 8 a.m.-1 p.m.

Hing Mau
1040 Maunakea St.
538-6544
Mon.-Sat. 8 a.m.-5 p.m.; Sun. 8 a.m.-3 p.m.

These two Chinese grocery stores on either side of Maunakea St. can supply you with everything you need for cooking your next nine-course Chinese dinner. Dried, bottled and canned foods, sauces, spices, herbs, noodles, tea, cooking implements—if you can't find it at one, the other is sure to have it. It's always a good idea to bring your cookbook along, especially if it has a Chinese glossary of food items, since English is sometimes limited in Chinatown stores.

H. A. S. R. Wine Co.
31 N. Pauahi St. next to Grand Cafe and Bakery
535-9463
Mon.-Fri. 10 a.m.-8 p.m.; Sat.,Sun. 10 a.m.-5 p.m.

A cozy, specialty wine store in the middle of Chinatown? An unusual find but a sign of the gentrifying of Chinatown, where boutiques, art galleries and restaurants are adding new life to this historic area. H. A. S. R. stands for Highly Allocated, Spoiled Rotten, the slogan for Mike and Terry Kakazu and their dream

wine shop. Select, allocated wines from small California wineries are their focus, and the Kakazus hope consumers will spoil themselves rotten with their selections. This is the perfect spot to find a bottle or two as you head to one of the area's restaurants.

Lee's Bakery and Kitchen

126 N. King St.
521-6261
Daily 5 a.m.-5 p.m.

Custard pie is a local favorite: light, creamy, slightly sweet custard in a flaky crust. And they say there is no better than Lee's custard pie.

Nam Fong

1029 Maunakea St.

599-5244

Mon.-Sat. 7 a.m.-4:30 p.m.; Sun. 7 a.m.-noon

The people in the line snaking out onto the sidewalk at this Chinatown institution are waiting for their roast duck, *pipa* duck or shoyu chicken. This shop's reputation for its roasted poultry is well known. And of course there's *char siu*, roast pork, spareribs and other items; whole roast pigs can be ordered, too.

Shung Chong Yuein

1027 Maunakea St.

531-1983

Mon.-Sat. 6 a.m.-4:30 p.m.; Sun. 6 a.m.-2 p.m.

Shung Chong Yuein is where Chinese come to buy special foods for Chinese celebrations: *gau* and candied fruits and vegetables for

Chinese New Year, moon cakes for the moon festival, wedding cakes for weddings. The Ng family, in business for over 40 years, makes all of these traditional Chinese sweets available throughout the year. Plus they make almond cookies, *char siu bao, joong, jin doi* and other Chinese delectables that are rarely made in a home kitchen. Unique here is the macadamia nut candy, a sticky, chewy bar of sesame seeds, sugar and macadamia nuts that's a wonderful snack.

Wah Wah Seafood

157 N. King St.
533-3283
Mon.-Sat. 6:30 a.m.-4:30 p.m.; Sun. 6:30 a.m.-1 p.m.

The many aquaculture farmers on Oʻahu find a ready market of people looking for live fresh fish and seafood products. When you want catfish, tilapia, grouper, abalone, shrimp and prawns, alive and kicking, this is the place to come. Kahuku shrimp and prawn farmers deliver here; abalone comes from the Big Island. There's also live Dungeness crab and Maine lobster (available at most seafood stores) and frogs.

Wing Loy Market

1036 Maunakea St.
523-5464
Mon.-Fri. 6:30 a.m.-4:30 p.m.; Sat. 6 a.m.-4:30 p.m.; Sun. 5:30
    a.m.-2 p.m.

When Nam Fong runs out of ducks and chickens, people cross the street and come here. But if you're looking for *char siu*, folks say it's better at Wing Loy than at Nam Fong. Only you can be the judge; just know that all is fresh and tasty on both sides of the street.

Yat Tung Chow Noodle Factory
150 N. King St.
531-7982
Mon.-Sat. 6 a.m.-3 p.m.; Sun. 6 a.m.-1 p.m.

Yat Tung Chow Noodle Factory is a wheat noodle factory owned and operated by the Chow family, who came to Hawai'i in 1976 from Canton, China. All sizes and shapes of noodles are made here—chow mein, thin chow mein, *udon*, flat egg noodle, elastic noodle, Shanghai noodle—as well as wrappers for *won ton, mundoo, gau gee, siu mai* and potstickers, each a different thickness. While you can find fresh noodles and wrappers in supermarkets, these are the freshest and best.

Ying Leong Look Funn Factory
1028 Kekaulike St.
537-4304
Mon.-Sat. 6:30 a.m.-3:30 p.m.; Sun. 6:30 a.m.–1:30 p.m.

For 40 years now, Fu Ying Chee, originally from Hong Kong, has operated this rice noodle factory that turns out about a thousand pounds of rice noodle sheets each day. You can watch the workers oiling pans that are filled with the rice noodle batter, which is then steamed to perfection, hand folded and stacked. Plain noodle sheets are sent off to restaurants that make fresh *chow fun* dishes. Shrimp and *char siu* speckle other sheets that are served in dim sum restaurants and eaten with soy sauce. This is one of Chinatown's treasures.

WHERE TO EAT IN CHINATOWN

Ba-Le Sandwich Shop
150 N. King St.
521-3973
Mon.-Sat. 6:30 a.m.-5 p.m.; Sun. 6:30 a.m.-4 p.m.

Thanh Quoc Lam emigrated from Vietnam in 1979. Four years later he opened his flagship Ba-le Sandwich Shop, introducing Honolulu food lovers to Vietnamese sandwiches: steamed pork or pate with pickled vegetables, cilantro and chili sauce in a freshly baked, crisp-crust baguette. The sandwich list has grown, Vietnamese specialties and desserts are served, and Ba-Le is known for its delicious baguettes and croissants. Lam, an award-winning businessman, has parlayed this one shop into a franchise with many locations on O'ahu and a bakery facility (see page 127) that caters to airlines and restaurants. But his shop in Chinatown is still the best.

Char Hung Sut (see page 31)

Grand Cafe and Bakery
31 N. Pauahi St.
531-0001
Breakfast and lunch Mon.-Fri. 6:30 a.m.-2 p.m.; Sat. 7:30 a.m.-
    1 p.m.; closed Sun.
Municipal parking lot and street parking

This spot is an oasis for comfort foods like meat loaf, braised short ribs, seafood chowder and fish and chips. Everything is house-made, including the corned beef used in a breakfast hash and lunchtime Reuben sandwich. Bearing the name of an early 1900s

Chinatown establishment, this gem is also known for great pastry and dessert offerings, from scones and croissants to apple pie, carrot cake, peanut butter banana cream tarts and luscious chocolate cake. A comfortable, casual spot with great eats; brunch menu on Saturday. Bring your own spirits; H. A. S. R. Wine Co. is next door.

✝ Indigo Eurasian Cuisine

1121 Nu'uanu Ave.
808 521-2900
Lunch Tues.-Fri. 11:30 a.m.-2 p.m.
Dinner Tues.-Sat. 6-9:30 p.m.
Closed Sun., Mon.
Valet and street parking

Few fine-dining restaurants exist in this part of Honolulu, known for its ethnic hole-in-the-wall eateries, shops, art galleries and grocery stores. At Indigo, an exotic tropical Asian ambiance sets the tone for this restaurant that is unique in its food repertoire: Chinese and Southeast Asian flavors with a contemporary twist.

Chef Glenn Chu learned to cook watching his Chinese grandmother, who regularly prepared meals for family gatherings. His mother was a baker, so he learned that side of the kitchen, too. After success with a fine French restaurant (RoxSan Patisserie) and a Moroccan restaurant (Hajji Baba), Chu finally opened a "Chinese" restaurant in Chinatown unlike any other. We're not talking typical stir-fried dishes and noodles, but goat cheese won tons, lobster potstickers, *liliko'i*-glazed sweet-and-sour baby back ribs, *kaffir* lime–scented pan-seared fish and steamed buns filled with eggplant and sun-dried tomato. Chu is a Chinese-inspired chef who has traveled through Europe, the United States and Asia and distilled the flavors, ingredients and techniques to make his own mark on the culinary scene, starting in 1994.

The location adds to the ambiance: Indigo's vitality extends beyond the dining room and the lush outdoor setting to the Green Room and Opium Den next door, which offer hip Honoluluans martinis, spirits and entertainment each night.

Legend Seafood Restaurant
Chinese Cultural Plaza
100 N. Beretania, Suite 108
532-1868
Dim sum and lunch Mon.-Fri. 10:30 a.m.-2 p.m.; Sat., Sun. 8
    a.m.-2 p.m.
Dinner daily 5:30-9 p.m.

As its name implies, this is a seafood restaurant. But we like it especially for its dim sum offerings during lunch: a wide variety of tasty morsels that will satisfy the hungry. Choose spinach and scallop, Shanghai or *har gow* dumplings from the steam cart; turnip cake and fried dumplings from the "fry" cart; rice noodle rolls from another; cold dishes and sweets from another. It's noisy, it's quick and there's little in the way of service. But it's quite delicious.

Little Village Noodle House
1113 Smith St.
545-3008
Sun.-Thurs. 10:30 a.m.-10:30 p.m.; Fri., Sat. 10:30 a.m.-midnight

There's nothing little about this modern, clean bistro-like restaurant that is big on service and flavorful food. No humdrum Chinese fare here: fresh spicy, garlicky green beans with pork, salted fish and chicken fried rice, stir-fried Shanghai *mochi* and tasty potstickers are only a few of the dishes one has to have.

Countless more plus many noodle and dumpling specialties will entice you back again and again. Take a peek at the kitchen action through the glass partition, be pleased by the western-style courteous service, bring your own beer, wine or spirits and enjoy the casual ambiance for lunch and dinner.

Mabuhay Cafe and Restaurant
1049 River St.
545-1956
Daily 10 a.m.-10 p.m.

In Chinatown, Filipino culture and cuisine are major influences. Many produce shops in the area stock the necessities for preparing this Spanish-Malay-Chinese cuisine. And Mabuhay has been serving these dishes for about 40 years in Honolulu: *pancit, lumpia, pinacbet, sarciado,* adobo and more under the watchful eyes of Filomena and Carmelita Lumauag. Once discovered, Filipino food can be quite addictive, and there's no better place to try it.

Mei Sum Chinese Dim Sum Restaurant
65 N. Pauahi St.
531-3268
Daily 7 a.m.-9 p.m.

This is a popular Chinatown spot for Hong Kong–style dim sum, starting early in the morning and going through dinnertime. There's a wide variety to choose from, brought to you on carts. In addition to the well-made standard fare—*char siu bao, siu mai, har gau,* etc.—do try their spinach and chive dumplings, lotus leaf–wrapped rice, steamed *mochi* rice dumplings and the soybean-wrapped bundles. There's a full menu of Chinese specialties, too.

Whatever you try, you won't be disappointed in the freshly made fare. Bring your own beer, wine or spirits.

Royal Kitchen (see page 33)

To Chau
1007 River St.
533-4549
Daily 8:30 a.m.-2:30 p.m.

Customers line up early in the day for a steaming bowl of *phô*, the specialty of this no-frills restaurant. Early is appropriate, since *phô* is breakfast fare in the land of its origin. You can order this North Vietnamese beef noodle soup a dozen different ways—including rare steak, tendon, brisket, tripe, and meatballs; there is even a version made with chicken broth. The soups are always freshly made since they run out by midafternoon and close. The To family runs this eatery that has been serving more than a couple of hundred bowls of *phô* a day for close to 20 years.

Wong Kwok Hometown Noodle House
2 N. Hotel St.
548-5888
Daily 8 a.m.-8 p.m.

The specialty here is *lai fun* (rice noodles—thick, silky, ropes in a flavorful broth or with a stir-fried topping). The noodles are made of rice flour and water by the drip method: they are dripped over a cauldron of boiling water to set their shape and texture. Try the braised duck with mountain yam or the noodles with fish ball and fish cake in broth. Or choose from several other preparations from a picture menu. Very satisfying.

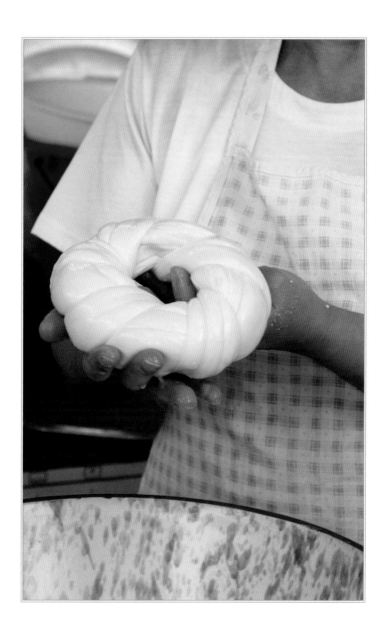

COOKING SCHOOLS
AND CLASSES

Cooking classes are one way of learning about a location's food culture. Unfortunately, most of the classes offered by the following organizations are mostly about restaurant food rather than "local food." But many of the chefs teaching the classes were born and raised here and can offer insights into island foodways. Best of all, the chefs do cook delicious food, often based on local food, so you'll end up learning a lot and enjoying some really good food.

Gourmet Cooking Hawaii
735-7788
www.gourmetcookinghawaii.com

This company engages chefs at top Honolulu restaurants to teach cooking classes in their restaurants. Classes are held on Saturday mornings, usually twice a month. The fee (usually $95) includes a three-hour demonstration class, a sampling of the dishes with wine pairings, a gift bag, a certificate of completion and recipes to take home. Groups can also organize private classes through Gourmet Cooking Hawaii.

Gros Bonnet
1431 S. Beretania St.
591-2708

Gros Bonnet means "tall hat," no doubt referencing a chef's toque, which you will undoubtedly wear as you complete the year-long culinary program here. This is a school focused on professional training for career-minded individuals. The curriculum is European based, intended to give students training in French culinary techniques, *garde manger,* baking and patisserie. The one-year program accepts students quarterly; instructors are active and retired chefs. Classes are held five hours a day, four days a week.

Kapi'olani Community College
4303 Diamond Head Road
734-9211
www.kcc.hawaii.edu

The state's seven community college campuses offer professional culinary training programs for wannabe chefs, with the largest facility at Kapi'olani Community College. Those who just want to learn for fun can take part in noncredit courses offered each semester on weekends and evenings. Chef instructors offer classes in baking and pastry, ethnic cuisines, and healthy and vegetarian cooking, as well as basic classes in cooking skills and techniques. Schedules are available on its website.

RESTAURANT AND HOTEL CLASSES

A few restaurants and hotels around town offer their own cooking classes, usually advertised to their customer mailing list or announced in local newspapers. These are not regular occurrences, so it's best to just check from time to time.

3660 on the Rise, with chef Russell Siu: usually two or three cooking classes a year in the evenings. Go to www.3660.com or call 737-1177.

Kahala Culinary Academy: The Kahala Mandarin Oriental Hawai'i hotel features Saturday morning classes in Hoku's restaurant that are open to all comers. The hotel's chefs take turns teaching a variety of topics, including pastry and dessert making. Call 739-8888.

Halekūlani Hotel: In the past this hotel has hosted Cordon Bleu chefs for weeklong hands-on cooking classes as well as guest chefs who do one-day demonstrations. Call 923-2311.

Hilton Hawaiian Village Resort: Occasional classes featuring the hotel's chefs or guests are staged; call 949-4321.

FOOD FESTIVALS AND EVENTS

Throughout the year, there are numerous food and cultural festivals where one can partake of the wide array of foods available in Honolulu. Some are one-day festivals celebrating an ethnic groups' heritage; others are multiday events featuring hotel and restaurant chefs cooking for a charitable cause. Dates change from year to year, so here's a list of what happens, with phone numbers to call for exact dates and times.

CHINESE NEW YEAR

The lunar new year is celebrated by the Chinese and Vietnamese communities sometime in January or February. It's a festive time in Chinatown, where shopkeepers offer a multitude of traditional decorations, paraphernalia and of course food treats in keeping with tradition. On the weekends before the lunar new year, Chinatown streets are closed so merchants and food vendors can set up booths as part of the celebration. Lion dances at night, punctuated by firecrackers, add to the festive time in Honolulu. For information, call the Chinese Chamber of Commerce, 533-3181.

MALASSADA DAY

Shrove Tuesday, the day before the beginning of the Christian Lenten season, is Malassada Day in Hawai'i. Head for Leonard's, Champion or Agnes' (see pages 30–40) to pick up a dozen on the way to work or just enjoy a few; church groups and other organizations often sell hot malassadas on this day. For information, call the Hawaii Council on Portuguese Heritage, 845-1616.

ST. PATRICK'S DAY CELEBRATION

Murphy's Bar and Grill always celebrates St. Patrick's Day in a big way. Traditional corned beef and cabbage, lamb shanks, Gaelic steak, fish 'n' chips, Irish stew and blarney burgers are usually on the menu. March 17 or a day close to it; call 531-0422.

WAIKĪKĪ SPAM® JAM

We really do love our Spam in Hawai'i and we celebrate it with an annual festival in Waikīkī. Spam memorabilia, crafts and musubi (rice ball) contests are part of the festivities staged by the Waikiki Improvement Association, usually in April. Call 923-1094.

HAWAII FARM BUREAU FEDERATION (HFBF) ANNUAL DINNER

Chef Roy Yamaguchi and farmer Dean Okimoto spearhead this annual grazing and sit-down dinner at Roy's Restaurant in Hawai'i Kai. Yamaguchi's chef pals are part of the lineup of fine food talent you'll find cooking at action stations next to wine and beer vendors. Upstairs in the restaurant itself, several other chef pals cook a multicourse dinner for high-ticket patrons. It's all in support of the activities of the HFBF, a nonprofit organization that supports farmers and agriculture in Hawai'i. Usually in June; for information, call 848-2074.

TASTE OF HONOLULU

Honolulu's biggest outdoor food event is held each June on the grounds of the Honolulu Civic Center (City Hall), featuring more than two dozen restaurants, beverage vendors and entertainment. It's a benefit for the Easter Seal Society, usually held Friday to Sunday. To attend, there's a nominal admission fee; then you buy scrip to purchase tasting-size portions from each of the vendors. It's an annual outdoor eat-a-thon. Call 536-1015 or go to www.taste808.com

MADE IN HAWAII FESTIVAL

A consumer showcase of food products made in Hawai'i plus lots of crafts, held each year in August at Blaisdell Center. There are always new food items, lots of samples and cooking demonstrations. Sponsored by the Hawaii Food Industry Association. Information: www.madeinhawaiifestival.com

SHOWCASE

The Honolulu Academy of Arts' Guild volunteers stage this annual food, wine and art benefit for education programs in August each year. Held in the outdoor courtyards of the building, this is a food lover's heaven, featuring the top dozen or so chefs in Honolulu and winemakers touting their best vintages. Creativity in food really displays itself here, and it's a lovely late summer grazing experience. Call 532-8700 or go to www.honoluluacademy.org

GREEK FESTIVAL

For over a quarter of a century, the small but spirited Greek community in Honolulu has celebrated its culture and food with an annual festival in August at Ala Moana Park. The ladies of Saints Constantine and Helen Greek Orthodox Cathedral prepare moussaka, spanakopita, baklava, *souvlaki* and other specialties; there's entertainment, dancing and lots of fun. For information, call 521-7220.

OKINAWAN FESTIVAL

An annual celebration of the Okinawan community, a major component of Hawai'i's ethnic mix dating back to the islands' plantation era. People love to go to this festival to get *andagi*, the deep-fried doughnut unique to this group, fried up by the thousands. Pork is an important part of the Okinawan diet, so the festival also features dishes like pig's feet and spareribs; noodles, *champuru* and sweet potato are usually served, too. This is a late summer festival; call 845-2255.

HONOLULU WINE FESTIVAL

This benefit for the Hawaii Lupus Foundation, held in September, is a gala wine-tasting event with many top Honolulu chefs participating. There's usually a formal sit-down dinner with a celebrity guest chef, too. Call 538-1522.

‘ILIMA AWARDS

Hawai‘i's best restaurants—voted upon by the readers of the *Honolulu Advertiser*—are honored in an onstage song-and-dance awards presentation by Honolulu's leading stage performers. A grand tasting of food prepared by the award winners follows, with lots of wines and spirits and dancing. A benefit for Diamond Head Theatre held annually in October at the theater. Call 733-0277.

HO‘OKIPA

Culinary students and faculty show off their talents and creations in this annual fund-raising event for the Culinary Arts and Hospitality and Tourism programs at Kapi‘olani Community College. Supporters get to enjoy the fruits of their labor, all served up in grand style. Call 734-9000.

HALE ‘ĀINA AWARDS

HONOLULU Magazine honors top restaurants in its January edition, and an awards party is held each year, attended by lots of folks in the Hawai‘i food and beverage industry and the foodie community. Award-winning chefs cook for their peers, showing off their best efforts. For more information call 537-9500.

DESSERT FANTASY

A dessert lover's dream event, with lots of chocolate for chocoholics, to benefit United Cerebral Palsy. November; call 532-6744.

FOOD LOVER'S FINDS

Hawaiʻi grows a lot of different foods—in fact, they say you can grow anything in Hawaiʻi if you find the right spot among the islands' geographic and climactic regions. Indeed, from sandy beach locales where coconut trees thrive to cooler elevations where stone fruit is prolific, Hawaiʻi is a year-round producer of fruits and vegetables. While we can't list everything Hawaiʻi grows, we can highlight some of the unique products grown here that enliven our food scene and make for delicious, healthy eating.

BEEF

Beef cattle were introduced to the islands in 1793 and soon became an important part of the islands' economy, traded as sailing ships came to the islands to replenish their supplies. Beef also became an important part of the local diet: beef stew is still very popular today, as is *pipikaula*, strips of dried seasoned beef also known as Hawaiian beef jerky.

Beef cattle are still raised today on Hawaiʻi, Maui and Oʻahu. But the cost of large open tracts of land for grazing and the cost of shipping feed to Hawaiʻi have made it uneconomical to finish beef in Hawaiʻi. Most ranchers ship their cattle to the mainland as calves, but a few raise their cattle on pasture without hormones and antibiotics, and their beef is available on their respective islands.

North Shore Cattle Co., in Haleʻiwa on Oʻahu, supplies prime cuts of its grass-finished beef to restaurants, and hamburger and sausages to supermarkets and specialty food stores. They are a presence at the Saturday Farmers' Market at KCC (see pages 109–111), as well as at other markets organized by the Hawaii Farm Bureau Federation. They also serve up burgers at the Dole Visitor Center in the middle of the pineapple fields on Oʻahu.

Kulana Beef from the island of Hawai'i and Maui Cattle Co. beef are other brands to look for in stores and restaurants.

Grass-fed beef tastes and chews differently: it is beefier in flavor and firmer in texture, with less marbling (fat). It may take getting used to, but its healthier qualities should cause food lovers to seek it out.

CHOCOLATE

A chocolate industry is beginning to grow on Hawaiian soil, producing the only chocolate grown in the United States. In the 1980s, commercial plantings of cacao began on the island of Hawai'i. But it wasn't until 2000 that Hawai'i's first chocolate was produced. The Original Hawaiian Chocolate Factory in Kona, Hawai'i, grows and processes cacao into milk and dark chocolate bars, using only Hawai'i-grown cacao beans that thrive within the cacao-growing belt, 20 degrees north and south of the equator.

While some say that blending Hawai'i chocolate with beans from elsewhere would improve the flavor of the chocolate, owners

Bob and Pam Cooper are committed to keeping their chocolate an all-Hawai'i product. Theirs is a good eating chocolate, especially their dark bar, which can also be used in baking and desserts. Since production is limited, it's not always easy to find this chocolate; check specialty food stores and the Saturday Farmers' Market at KCC.

COFFEE

The only place in the United States that grows coffee is Hawai'i. It has been grown commercially on the island of Hawai'i since the mid-1800s, mostly in the Kona area, where Hawai'i's reputation for coffee is renowned.

Kona coffee, an arabica bean, is still grown in the rocky soil of dry upland areas 500 to 2,500 feet above sea level on the island of Hawai'i. The climate and soil produce a mild, flavorful coffee with unique characteristics. Today's estate producers still hand pick their coffee cherries, roast their dried beans in small batches and

market to a sophisticated coffee-consuming clientele. One hundred percent Kona coffee is indeed unique; Kona blends contain a minimum of 10 percent Kona-grown coffee.

Other coffees are grown in Hawai'i, too. Kaua'i, Moloka'i and O'ahu have their own proprietary coffees, distinctive in their flavor, reflecting the climate and geography of their growing areas. Food lovers can find these coffees, pure and blended, at coffee shops in Honolulu as well as in supermarkets and specialty shops.

CORN

Corn in Hawai'i is supersweet. The No. 10 variety is cultivated throughout the state, a crunchy ear with small, very sweet kernels. Developed at the University of Hawai'i, this corn is available year-round, but it is especially prolific during the summer months. The North Shore of O'ahu is particularly known for its sweet corn.

You'll often find ears lopped off at the top, a way to rid the ear of a pesky caterpillar that would like to eat the kernels before you do. Find sweet corn at roadside stands, farmers' markets and occasionally at supermarkets.

GINGER

Hawai'i grows some of the best ginger in the world. Ginger is a rhizome, a creeping horizontal stem that grows beneath the surface of the soil. Most of it grows along the Hāmākua Coast of the island of Hawai'i, and it is exported everywhere. Of course, we see it in our markets. Be on the lookout for young ginger around August and September: young ginger has less fiber and a milder flavor, making it perfect for pickling.

"HAWAIIAN" SALT

Salt is the most basic and important of all seasonings and flavor enhancers in cooking. It is such an essential part of the development of cuisine and the preservation of food throughout history that it also brought power and wealth to those who could harvest and trade it.

Early Hawaiians gathered *pa'akai*, Hawaiian for salt, at the shorelines around the islands. It was traded when sailors came to call on the Hawaiian Islands and it was used to preserve foods, especially beef, which became another important trade item. For the Hawaiians, salt was also a purifying agent, used to bless new structures or canoes, thrown over the shoulder before entering a house or used in ceremonial bathing following a funeral.

Today, "Hawaiian salt" refers to a coarse sea salt that actually comes from California. It is a white salt, used for cooking and seasoning. *'Alaea* is Hawaiian salt colored pink by the addition of a red clay from the island of Kaua'i. Both are sold in markets throughout the state.

True Hawaiian salt gathered from Hawaiian shores is available in some specialty food stores. Hawai'i Kai Salt is one brand, harvested from Moloka'i shores and offered as white, *'alaea,* and black (charcoal) salts. Another is Kona Salt, obtained from the desalination of water from 2,000 feet below the surface at Keāhole on the island of Hawai'i.

If you happen to be on Kaua'i during the summer months, you will find families who harvest salt as they have done for generations at the Salt Ponds at Hanapēpē. Befriending one of the salt gatherers might get you some clear white flaky salt that has a sweet quality to it. And being there will enable you to witness an ancient way of salt gathering that is as unique as that of the *paludiers* of the Brittany coast of France.

HEARTS OF PALM

If you've ever eaten a heart of palm, it probably came from a can and was a white spear flavored by its brining solution. A fresh heart of palm is quite different: mild flavored, crisp and silky, reminiscent of an artichoke heart.

The heart of the peach palm is cultivated along the Hāmakua Coast of the island of Hawai'i. Trees form a multistemmed clump, and each clump is managed to produce a stalk for harvest each year. At about six to eight feet in height, the stalks are harvested by hand and the outer layers are stripped away to get at the heart.

Hearts of palm can be used in salads or sautéed in a little olive oil. Fine restaurants in Honolulu serve them, and they can be found fresh at the Saturday Farmers' Market at KCC.

HONEY

With all the agriculture in Hawai'i, honey is an important crop. Pollination for many seed crops depends on active honey beehives, where the sweet nectar we enjoy is produced. Not only does Hawai'i produce a lot of honey, but it also cultivates queen bees for export.

Honey takes on the flavor characteristics of the trees that honeybees visit, like macadamia nut, *'ōhi'a lehua,* and *kiawe.* Unique among honeys is Volcano Island Honey, a whitish cream honey gathered from bees that frequent *kiawe* trees on the island of Hawai'i. Look for Hawai'i honey at supermarkets, specialty food stores and farmers' markets.

MACADAMIA NUTS

The creamy, buttery macadamia nut was introduced to Hawai'i in the early 1870s from Australia. It has been in commercial production since 1948, mostly in the Puna and Ka'ū districts of the island of Hawai'i. Honoka'a is a center for macadamia nut processing.

The majestic macadamia nut tree yields nuts after seven years. The tough shell of the nut must be cracked under great pressure without crumbling the nut. The nuts are roasted, seasoned or flavor-coated with savory and sweet concoctions. For baking, buy diced nuts, since the nuts tend to shard when cut. Macadamia nuts are found throughout Hawai'i.

Macadamia nut oil, pressed from the raw nut, is a pale golden oil that can be used in cooking. It has a high smoke point and has been shown to be healthier than other oils, including olive oil. Like other nut oils, macadamia nut oil has a pronounced flavor that must be considered when you use it in cooking. Mauna Loa and Oils of Aloha are two brands available in island stores.

NALO GREENS

You'll see "Nalo Greens" on many a restaurant menu around Honolulu. It's a proprietary blend created by farmer Dean Okimoto of Nalo Farms, known as "farmer to the chefs." It's a soft-textured mesclun mixture that has a spicy and bitter note and colorful palette.

In the Nalo Greens mixture are arugula, mizuna, *tatsoi,* red mustard, red Russian kale, peppercress, tango, green and red oak lettuce, red and green romaine and beet greens. Since these are delicate greens, they are best dressed with a light vinaigrette or simply with olive oil and salt.

Nalo Greens are sold primarily to restaurants and are available at Hawaii Farm Bureau Federation farmers' markets. Nalo Greens and another mixture called Dean's Greens are becoming more available at supermarkets.

SUGAR

Sugar was king for nearly two centuries in Hawai'i, the product of sugar cane grown on thousands of acres of land on all islands. Only two plantations remain today, on Maui and Kaua'i, growing the tall stalks of green that undulated in the trade winds and gave rise to a thriving economy in the middle of the Pacific.

Hawai'i's sugar is processed by the C&H Refinery in California, as it has been for many years. But Hawaiian Commercial and Sugar Co. on Maui, growers of sugar cane, process raw sugar into white raw sugar and tubinado sugar. White raw sugar is coarser than granulated and has a hint of molasses. Turbinado is even coarser and has a decidedly brown color as a result of its molasses content. Both can be used on the table or in baked goods like cookies, muffins and quick breads. Both are truly Hawai'i-grown products, available in all supermarkets.

TROPICAL FRUITS

Tropical fruits are among Hawai'i's bounty: papaya, pineapple, banana, mango, lychee, rambutan, star fruit, guava, passion fruit, citrus of all kinds, cherimoya, sapote, durian, jackfruit. Add loquat, persimmons, figs, pomegranates and countless other exotic fruits.

While some are available year-round, others are seasonal. Some are produced in backyards; others, on a commercial scale.

Some can be found in supermarkets; others, only at farmers' markets or from a friendly neighbor. Food lovers should note the seasons for these fruits and search them out.

> Spring: loquat, mountain apple, starfruit, soursop
> Summer: avocado, dragon fruit, jackfruit, longan, lychee, mango, passion fruit, strawberry guava, *pohā*, pomelo
> Autumn: guava, *mamey sapote*, *ʻōhelo* berry, rambutan, starfruit
> Winter: atemoya, cherimoya, durian, fig, kumquat, loquat, mangosteen, persimmon

Another way to enjoy these exotic taste treats is in jams, jellies and preserves made by local food manufacturers. There are many who take pride in harvesting and processing local fruit into delicious products made in small batches. Some of the most popular products are passion fruit curd, mango chutney, guava jam, pineapple chutney, dried persimmons, and guava, passion fruit and papaya seed salad dressings. The best place to find these items is at the Saturday Farmers' Market at KCC and at specialty food stores.

Avocados

Over 200 varieties of avocado grow in Hawai'i. Some, like the Sharwill, are commercially cultivated; most are the product of backyard trees or small farms. Locally grown avocados can be small ovals or large round balls; the flesh can be creamy or stringy; the flavor can be watered down or very nutty. Puzzling as they may seem, Hawai'i's avocados are very flavorful. Look for avocados at markets throughout Honolulu and especially at farmers' markets.

Bananas

Most local folks won't eat those big bananas from South America. We like our apple bananas, short, fat and sweet, with a slight tartness that makes them just the best banana around. Well, there is the Williams banana, also grown here, that comes close. But apple bananas are so much better than imported ones, and once they turn yellow (ripe), they stay firm for a few days. For the best prices on apple bananas—they can cost 50 percent more than imported bananas—shop at farmers' markets and Chinatown stores.

Mangoes

Of all the tropical fruits, the mango is the most divine. This golden orb of juicy, sweet flesh with a hint of tartness is unlike any other, especially in Hawai'i. Taste mangoes in Southeast Asia or India or buy one of those South American varieties we see in our supermarkets and you realize that Hawai'i's mangoes are the most delicious, most luscious fruit around.

How to eat a mango? Perfectly ripe and cold, over the kitchen

PICKLED MANGO

The first sign of mango season is the pickled mango signs along Oʻahu roads. Green mangoes are sliced and pickled, their natural color on display or with red food coloring added. Either way, pickled mango is a treat, surpassed only by perfectly luscious and ripe mangoes to come.

3 cups green mango slices
10 *li hing mui*
2 cups sugar
1 cup rice vinegar
1/4 cup Hawaiian salt

Put mango slices and *li hing mui* in a clean jar. Combine remaining ingredients in a saucepan and bring to a boil. Cool to lukewarm. Pour over mangoes. Let stand for 24 hours and then store in the refrigerator.

sink to catch the juices running down your arms and chin as you savor its freshness and flavor. Consider the qualities of the mango you're devouring: creamy flesh or slightly stringy, mostly sweet or sweet with a little sourness, firm or soft? Focus on its flavor: hints of peach, pear, pineapple, melon, blackberry, cherry, green apple, papaya, apricot, cinnamon? Remember all these characteristics and then note the variety you're eating. Become a mango snob, asking for a mango by its name: Haden, Pirie, Mapulehu, Tommy Atkins, Sun Gold, Keitt, Waianae Beauty, Manzanilla.

Small common and Chinese mangoes are the best for making mango chutney; pickled mangoes crop up along rural roads, and mango bread is one of the most delicious ways to use up an abundant supply of this fruit.

The mango season is all too brief: it begins around May and may extend into September. There are only a few commercial mango farms in the state; most mangoes come from backyard trees. Befriending someone with a mango tree is a good thing.

Papaya

Papaya is the breakfast fruit of choice in Hawai'i. Called *hei* in Hawaiian, this orangey yellow fruit is a good source of vitamins A and C, and it contains papain, a natural protein-splitting enzyme that is used to tenderize meats.

Many varieties of papaya are available at all markets throughout Hawai'i. Red-fleshed Sunrise grows particularly well on Kaua'i; bulbous, round X77 grows well on O'ahu's North Shore. On Hawai'i, the Puna or Kapoho papaya, also known as the Solo papaya, is the most prolific. Most papaya farmers are on Hawai'i, the center of Hawai'i's papaya export industry.

SunUp, Rainbow and Laie Gold papayas are genetically modified papayas developed to resist the ringspot virus that once crippled the papaya industry.

All varieties can be found at supermarkets, neighborhood grocery stores, farmers' markets and roadside stands throughout Hawai'i. Finding the variety you like is important, since each has different flavors and textures. Solo and Rainbow papayas are the standard bearers for papayas: sweet, with firm-textured orangey flesh and mild aroma. Sunrise and SunUp are red-fleshed and sweet, but tend to be soft in texture and don't have the aroma that some people find distracting. Laie Gold and X77 are firm fleshed, with a cantaloupe-like texture and sweetness.

The best way to enjoy papaya is halved with a squeeze of lemon or lime. Hollowed-out papayas are often used to serve chicken or shrimp salads. Papaya seed dressing is also popular.

Pineapple

Next to sugar, pineapple was Hawai'i's second most important crop in the 20th century. Native to South America, pineapple made its way to Hawai'i via Spanish sailing ships. But it was the marketing savvy of James Dole and William Eames, founders of Dole and Del Monte Pineapple, that made the fruit synonymous with Hawai'i.

Because pineapples are picked ripe, they could not be shipped the long distance to markets on the U.S. mainland. Dole decided to can pineapple and established the infrastructure. Many an old-timer in Honolulu has a story about working in the pineapple cannery during summer breaks from school.

Today, with air transportation, fresh pineapple is shipped to markets everywhere, though there is much competition from other growing areas in the world. The Gold pineapple is the newest standard bearer for sweetness, but look for seasonal white Sugarloaf pineapples from Kaua'i and Sweet Gold pineapples from the island of Hawai'i for sweetness with pineappley flavor.

VANILLA

The pod of an orchid plant, the vanilla bean is another of Hawai'i's unique agricultural products. The orchid must be pollinated during the few hours that its flower opens in order to produce a pod that must be picked, dried and cured to produce a fragrant, pliable vanilla bean prized in culinary preparations.

The Hawaiian Vanilla Company, headquartered on the island of Hawai'i, grows and produces vanilla beans, extract and body lotion for retail sale. Look for it at specialty food stores and the Saturday Farmers' Market at KCC.

aburage Japanese for thin deep-fried tofu or bean curd.

adobo Filipino preparation of chicken or pork marinated and cooked in vinegar, garlic, peppercorns and bay leaves.

ʻahi Yellowfin, or bigeye, tuna, red fleshed with firm texture and beefy flavor, usually eaten raw.

ʻahi katsu Preparation featuring ʻahi that is breaded in *panko* and deep-fried.

aioli French for garlicky mayonnaise of Provence.

ʻalaea Hawaiian word for coarse salt mixed with red clay from Kauaʻi.

andagi Okinawan fried doughnut leavened with baking powder.

arroz caldo Filipino chicken-rice soup.

atemoya Green, rough-skinned fruit with a sweet custardlike cream-colored pulp and black seeds. A cross between a cherimoya and sweetsop.

azuki beans Small red beans used in Japanese cooking; they are often used in confections, pounded into a paste and sweetened with sugar.

baba ghanoush Middle Eastern purée of eggplant, usually seasoned with garlic, lemon and olive oil.

bento Japanese portable boxed meal, usually consisting of rice, pickles and chicken, beef or fish.

bibingka Filipino baked confection made of glutinous rice flour, coconut milk and brown sugar. Similar to *mochi* and *gau.*

boiled peanuts Local preparation of peanuts, soaked in a brine and boiled; eaten as a snack.

bouillabaisse French stew from Provence, made with an assortment of seafood and fish, tomatoes and other seasonings.

calamansi Small, very tart citrus often used in Filipino cookery. Also known as *calamondin.*

carnitas Mexican preparation of pork, well cooked and browned.

champuru Okinawan dish of stir-fried vegetables and tofu.

chanko nabe Japanese soup made with chicken, vegetables, fish and tofu eaten with onion-flavored soy sauce and vinegar. A traditional dish enjoyed by sumo wrestlers.

char siu Chinese barbecued pork, seasoned with soy sauce and five-spice and usually colored red.

char siu bao Chinese steamed or baked bun filled with diced *char siu.*

chazuke Tea-flavored rice, also flavored with bits of *nori,* pickled plums or other ingredients, favored at the end of a Japanese meal.

cherimoya Custard apple; leatherlike green-skinned fruit with a sweet, low-acid flesh and black seeds.

chichidango Soft, sweet *mochi* cut into rectangular strips, usually colored pink and white.

chimichanga Mexican burrito (tortilla wrapped around a filling) that is fried or deep-fried and usually garnished with salsa, guacamole, sour cream and shredded cheese.

chow fun Chinese stir-fried rice noodles.

chow mein Chinese stir-fried thin egg and wheat noodles.

ciabatta Italian "slipper" bread, long and thin, with a crisp crust and soft interior.

cone sushi See *inari* sushi.

crack seed Genre of fruits like cherries, plums, apricots, mangoes and olives, dried and preserved with sugar, salt, star anise and other seasonings. A favorite snack food in Hawai'i, sweet, salty, sour crack seed is mostly imported from Asia.

daifuku Japanese *mochi* filled with coarse *azuki* beans.

dashi Japanese stock made from seaweed and fish.

dim sum Chinese dumplings and specialties, steamed, baked or fried, served with tea for breakfast and lunch.

dinuguan Filipino dish of meat, intestines and pork blood.

dolmas Middle Eastern grape leaves filled with ground lamb, rice, onions, currants, pine nuts and seasonings.

donburi Japanese bowl of rice topped with chicken, fish, meat, eggs and/or vegetables. *Don* also refers to other dishes served in bowls.

dosai Flat bread of South India made of fermented ground rice and lentils.

duk Korean rice cakes, similar to *mochi,* eaten in soup or as a snack.

duk kook Korean rice cakes in soup.

durian Southeast Asian fruit with a spiky, brownish green skin and custardlike sweet flesh that is very pungent.

enchilada Mexican preparation in which a tortilla is wrapped around meat or cheese and served hot in a chile and tomato-based sauce.

epazote Pungent herb used fresh or dried in Mexican cookery, especially with beans.

filo Greek paper-thin pastry dough used in sweet and savory preparations.

foie gras French for "fat liver," referring to goose or duck liver, eaten as a pate or sliced and seared.

fried rice Leftover rice stir-fried with bits of meat, vegetables and seasonings.

furikake Japanese condiment of seaweed bits, sesame seeds, salt and seafood flavors, usually sprinkled on top of rice.

gau Chinese steamed confection of glutinous rice flour, sugar and water, usually made for the lunar new year.

gau gee Chinese rectangular dumplings filled with seafood, pork or other ingredients, served in broth or deep-fried.

gobo Japanese for burdock, a root eaten as a vegetable. Also refers to the dish of julienne-cut burdock prepared with carrot, soy sauce, sugar and other seasonings, also known as *kinpira gobo.*

guacamole Mexican dish of avocado, tomato, onion and garlic, usually served with tortilla chips.

guisantes Filipino dish of pork, peas, tomatoes and peppers.

HRC See Hawai'i Regional Cuisine

habutai Japanese *mochi* with strained *azuki* bean filling.

half-moon Half-round steamed dumpling filled with meat or seafood and vegetables; one of many dim sum.

halo halo Filipino "mix mix," a concoction of shaved ice, sweet beans, fruit, gelatin cubes and other ingredients drizzled with sweetened condensed milk or evaporated milk.

hamachi Japanese yellowtail or amberjack fish, usually eaten raw as sashimi or in sushi.

haole Caucasian person.

har gow Steamed shrimp dumpling, one of many dim sum.

hash Local term for corned beef hash patties.

haupia Hawaiian coconut pudding thickened with arrowroot or cornstarch.

Hawai'i Regional Cuisine Term coined in the late 1980s for the "new cuisine" of Hawai'i, encompassing the use of fresh local ingredients and flavors in the cooking of the islands.

hei Hawaiian for papaya.

hoisin Chinese sweet, spicy sauce made of soybeans, garlic and spices.

huli huli Hawaiian for turn quickly, usually referring to chicken cooking on a grill.

hum hee Chinese salted fish.

hummus Middle Eastern sauce of mashed chickpeas, garlic, lemon juice and olive oil, usually served with pita.

ikura Japanese term for salmon roe.

imu Hawaiian underground oven or pit in which food is cooked.

inamona Hawaiian condiment of roasted and ground *kukui,* or candlenut.

inari sushi Japanese sushi preparation of seasoned rice with bits of gobo, carrot and green bean, stuffed into a pocket of *aburage*; also known as cone sushi.

izakaya Japanese tavern or pub serving drinks and a variety of small dishes.

jackfruit Large, spiny, oblong tropical fruit with a sweet golden flesh and seeds. The fruit can weigh up to a hundred pounds.

jin doi Chinese fried rice ball made of glutinous rice flour with a sweet filling in the hollow interior.

joong Chinese triangular steamed ti leaf–wrapped bundle of glutinous rice, pork, shrimp, duck egg, mushrooms and seasonings.

juhn Korean preparation of sliced meat, fish or vegetables, lightly floured, dipped in egg and fried.

Kaffir lime Tropical citrus with a bumpy, wrinkled skin, prized for its dark green glossy leaves that impart a unique flavor to Southeast Asian dishes.

kaiseki Formal Japanese meal.

kal bi Korean short ribs, marinated in soy sauce, garlic, sesame oil and other seasonings, usually cooked on a grill.

kālua pork Traditional Hawaiian preparation of smoky, well-cooked pork, in which a whole pig is roasted in an *imu*.

kamaboko Japanese fish cake, eaten plain or used in an assortment of dishes, made from fish paste and a thickener and steamed. Often colored pink.

kampachi Fish with an oily and tasty flesh. It is a cousin to *hamachi*.

kare kare Filipino oxtail casserole thickened with chopped peanuts.

kataifi Shredded filo dough.

katsu Japanese term for meat, fish or chicken coated with egg and breadcrumbs and deep-fried.

kau yuk Chinese preparation of braised pork belly.

keem pahb A seaweed-wrapped roll of rice filled with seasoned beef, vegetables and egg; a Korean "sushi."

kiawe Hawaiian for algaroba tree; its wood is used as charcoal and burns hot like mesquite.

kim chee Korean pickled vegetables seasoned with garlic and chili peppers.

ko chu jang Korean chili paste made of fermented soybean paste and chili peppers, eaten as a condiment or used in cooking.

Kona coffee Arabica coffee grown in the Kona area of the island of Hawai'i.

kook soo Korean dish of noodles in a well-seasoned hot or cold broth.

kūlolo Steamed or baked Hawaiian pudding of grated taro, sugar and coconut milk.

lai fun Chinese rice noodles.

lassi Indian chilled drink made with yogurt, flavored with fruit and spices.

lau lau Hawaiian dish of taro leaves, pork and salted butterfish wrapped in ti leaves and steamed.

lavosh Armenian cracker bread with sesame seeds, popular in Hawai'i restaurant bread baskets.

lechon Filipino roasted pig, usually cooked over an open spit, seasoned with lemongrass and garlic.

li hing mui The most distinguished and enduring of crack seed, this "traveler's plum" is sweet, salty and sour. It comes dry and wet, and its flavor, in powdered or liquid form, is applied to dried fruits and candies and used in baking, cooking and even in ice cream.

liliko'i Hawaiian word for passion fruit, a tropical fruit that is egg shaped and yellow or purple skinned, with a pulpy flesh dotted with black seeds. The sweet-sour flavor is distinctive and seductive.

limu Hawaiian word for plants living in water, usually referring to edible seaweed, or *ogo*.

loco moco A local dish of rice, seasoned ground beef patty, egg and brown gravy.

lomi lomi salmon Diced salted salmon, tomatoes and onions are worked and mixed with the fingers to produce a refreshing salad.

longan Southeast Asian fruit also known as dragon's eye. It is about an inch in diameter with a thin brown shell and translucent white flesh surrounding a black seed. It has a perfumy scent and sweet, mild flavor. A relative of lychee and rambutan.

longanisa Spanish pork sausage flavored with garlic, oregano and paprika, a favorite on the Filipino table.

lū'au Hawaiian feast or celebration. Also refers to the leafy tops of the taro plant, used in *lau lau* or cooked into a rich stew flavored with coconut milk.

lumpia Filipino fried spring roll, usually filled with pork and vegetables and encased in a thin egg-and-wheat-flour crepe.

lup cheong Chinese sausage that is reddish in color and savory sweet in flavor.

lychee Southeast Asian fruit with a rough red exterior and creamy white flesh surrounding a black seed. The fruit is juicy and sweet; it is in season during the summer months.

mahimahi Dolphinfish, or dorado.

maki sushi Japanese sushi that is rolled, usually in a sheet of nori, using a bamboo mat.

malassada Portuguese fried doughnuts without a hole, made with eggs and yeast and rolled in sugar. Contemporary versions have fillings like *haupia,* chocolate or Kona coffee cream.

manapua Local term for baked or steamed buns filled with *char siu* as well as the genre of local-style dim sum that includes half-moons, *pepeiao* and pork hash.

mandoo Korean dumplings of pork and/or beef, tofu and vegetables in a pastalike wrapper, crimped at the edges. Served in a broth with condiments or fried.

manju Japanese baked pastry filled with sweet *azuki* bean or lima bean paste. Newer versions include sweet potato and taro fillings.

mirin Japanese sweet cooking wine.

miso Japanese fermented soybean paste. Koreans call it *twaen jang.*

misoyaki Miso flavored and grilled, a common preparation for butterfish.

mochi Japanese rice cake made of glutinous rice that is steamed, pounded to a paste and then shaped into discs. Mochi can be plain or filled with sweetened beans or other fillings, eaten as a snack or served in soup. Local versions include butter, coconut and chocolate mochi, usually baked, and *chichidango*.

mochiko Rice flour made from glutinous rice, used in cooking and baking. A common preparation is *mochiko* chicken, chicken coated in *mochiko* and deep-fried.

moi Hawaiian name for threadfish, an esteemed fish among Hawaiians. Today it is raised in aquaculture ponds and in open ocean cages. Its white flesh is delicate and moist and it is best prepared whole, steamed or fried crisp.

musubi Japanese rice ball, triangular in shape with something of strong flavor in the center, like a pickled plum; it is wrapped in *nori* or sprinkled with sesame seeds.

naan East Indian flat bread made of white flour and yogurt, leavened with yeast, usually made in a tandoor oven.

nabemono Japanese term for one-pot dish, usually cooked at the table and served from the pot.

naeng myun Korean dish of noodles and garnishes in a cold broth.

Nalo Greens A delicate and spicy mix of baby greens grown at Nalo Farm in Waimānalo, Oʻahu. In the proprietary mix are arugula, mizuna, *tatsoi,* red mustard, red Russian kale, peppercress, tango, green and red oak lettuce, green and red romaine and beet greens.

namasu Japanese dish of seafood and vegetables seasoned with vinegar.

nishime Japanese stew of pork, vegetables and seaweed.

nori Japanese word for thin sheets of dried seaweed, often used to make sushi rolls or musubi.

ogo A type of *limu* or edible seaweed, reddish in color.

'ohana Hawaiian word for family.

'ōhelo Hawaiian native cranberry, found near the volcano on the island of Hawai'i.

okazu ya Japanese delicatessen.

onaga Red snapper with a delicate, tender, mild-flavored flesh.

ong choy Chinese for water spinach, a leafy green with arrowhead-shaped leaves. Also known as swamp cabbage, it is eaten raw or stir-fried.

'ono Hawaiian for delicious.

opakapaka Hawaiian name for snapper with a firm light pink flesh that is smooth and mild.

'ōpihi Hawaiian limpet harvested from rocky coastlines and eaten raw. It has a briny flavor.

oyako don Japanese *donburi* with chicken and eggs.

pa'akai Hawaiian for salt.

pad Thai Noodle dish of Thailand made with rice noodles, egg, shrimp, bean sprouts, chives, fish sauce, chili pepper and other ingredients.

paella Spanish preparation of rice flavored with saffron, cooked with seafood, fish, chicken, sausage, vegetables and other seasonings.

pandan Green leaves of screwpine, used in Southeast Asian cooking, especially to flavor rice dishes and confections.

pan de sal Filipino baked roll, slightly sweet.

paneer Fresh cheese used in a variety of East Indian preparations.

panini Italian "small bread," usually filled with meats and cheese.

panko Japanese breadcrumbs, coarse or fine in texture, used to coat foods to be deep-fried.

panna cotta Italian "cooked cream," a silky gelled cream usually served with fruit.

pancit Filipino noodle dish with meat, seafood or vegetables. The noodles are wheat or rice flour noodles.

pao duce Portuguese sweet bread, rich with eggs.

pastele Puerto Rican steamed grated banana surrounding seasoned pork, olives and tomato sauce; like a Mexican tamale.

pate French preparation of ground meat with a smooth or coarse texture, served hot or cold.

pau hana Hawaiian for "finished work" or end of workday.

pepeiao Hawaiian for "ear," used to identify a steamed *manapua* dumpling shaped like an ear.

phô Vietnamese beef noodle soup garnished with bean sprouts, basil, chili peppers and other seasonings. It is of North Vietnamese origin and usually eaten for breakfast or lunch.

pinacbet Filipino dish of vegetables and shrimp.

pipa duck Roasted flattened duck named for a Chinese musical instrument.

pipikaula Hawaiian dried beef, seasoned with salt or soy sauce and chili pepper. It's a Hawaiian-style beef jerky.

pita Middle Eastern flat bread with a pocket for stuffing.

pohā Hawaiian for cape gooseberry, a small, round, yellow-orange fruit with many seeds. It has a sweet-tart flavor; it is eaten raw, cooked in sauces or made into preserves.

poi Hawaiian starch staple of cooked taro, mashed into a smooth paste. It is bland but takes on a sour taste as it ages.

poke Hawaiian for "cut into pieces," the term refers to a dish of bite-size seasoned morsels of fish, seafood or anything else.

pork hash One of several types of *manapua* bearing a close resemblance to *siu mai,* a Chinese steamed pork dumpling.

povi masima Salt beef, usually a brisket of beef soaked in brine. It is well liked in the Samoan community, where it is boiled in several changes of water to take away the saltiness and then cooked with vegetables like cabbage.

pul ko gi Korean beef slices marinated in soy sauce, garlic, green onions and sesame oil and then cooked on a grill.

pūpū Hawaiian word for appetizer or hors d'oeuvre.

quesadilla Mexican preparation of tortillas and cheese cooked on a griddle; a Mexican grilled cheese sandwich.

rambutan Tropical fruit from Malaysia. It has bright-red rind with bristles. The sweet flesh is translucent white surrounding a single seed. A relative of the lychee.

ramen Japanese dish of wheat noodles served in broth.

risotto Italian rice dish prepared by adding hot stock to a starchy variety of rice, resulting in a creamy texture but separate and firm grains of rice. Vegetables, seafood, meat and cheeses are sometimes added.

saimin Hawai'i dish of Chinese noodles and steaming hot Japanese broth, traditionally topped with *char siu,* luncheon meat or *kamaboko* and green onions.

sake Japanese rice wine.

samosa Indian pastry filled with vegetables and other ingredients.

sarciado Filipino preparation of meat or seafood, thickened with eggs.

sashimi Japanese raw fish and shellfish.

saté Indonesian dish of skewered grilled meat, fish or poultry served with a spicy peanut-flavored sauce.

see mui Chinese term for crack seed.

senbei Japanese cookies, thin and crisp, in various flavors.

shabu-shabu Japanese *nabemono,* or one-pot dish, in which vegetables and beef are cooked in broth.

Shanghai dumpling A steamed pork dumpling with a spiral top, which, when you bite into it, delivers a mouthful of broth along with the savory pork filling.

A specialty of Shanghai, China, and dim sum restaurants.

shave ice Local term for finely shaved ice flavored with sweet fruit syrup.

shiso Japanese herb also known as perilla or beefsteak herb. It is related to mint and is often used in sushi.

shoyu Japanese word for soy sauce.

siu mai Steamed pork dumpling, a type of Chinese dim sum.

song pyun Korean steamed rice dumplings filled with sweet beans and sesame seeds.

souvlaki Greek specialty of grilled marinated lamb on skewers.

Spam *musubi* Hawai'i preparation of rice with a slice of Spam, wrapped in a strip of nori.

sukiyaki Japanese *nabemono,* or one-pot dish, in which beef and vegetables are cooked in a shallow pan and seasoned with soy sauce and sugar. Each bite is dipped in raw egg and eaten.

sushi Seasoned rice served with fresh raw fish or seafood or prepared in rolls with nori.

tabbouleh Middle Eastern dish of bulgur wheat, parsley, tomatoes, onions, mint, olive oil and lemon juice, served cold or at room temperature.

taco Mexican dish of folded crisp or soft tortillas, filled with beef, pork, fish or chicken and garnished with salsa, guacamole, cheese or other ingredients.

taegu Korean preparation of shredded codfish or cuttlefish, seasoned with honey and chili pepper.

tako Japanese for octopus.

tamale Mexican dish of masa, or corn flour dough, filled with meat, vegetables or cheese, wrapped in corn husks and steamed.

tartare A preparation of raw food, usually beef, as in steak or beef tartare. It also refers to raw fish or other uncooked foods.

tataki Japanese preparation of *aku,* or bonito, grilled on the outside but raw inside, served with a dipping sauce.

teishoku Japanese term for a set menu.

tempura Japanese preparation of vegetables and seafood dipped in a batter and deep-fried to lacy, crisp perfection.

teriyaki Japanese flavoring of soy sauce, mirin (cooking wine), sake and sugar applied to beef, chicken and other foods. The foods are usually grilled and basted with the marinade to achieve flavor and a shiny appearance.

ti Plant with long, green leaves often used as wrappers in food preparations.

tobiko Japanese for flying-fish roe, usually tiny, crunchy bright-orange bits. Sometimes you will see green *tobiko* that is flavored with wasabi.

tortilla Mexican round, unleavened flat bread, made from corn or wheat flour, eaten plain or filled or fried crisp.

tsumami Japanese green *mochi* with lima bean paste.

tzatziki Greek sauce of yogurt, cucumber, mint, garlic and olive oil served as a dip with pita or condiment for grilled meats or sandwiches.

'uala Hawaiian for sweet potato.

udon Japanese wheat noodles, soft and thick.

wasabi Japanese green horseradish, pungent, served with sashimi and sushi. The powdered form is colored horseradish; fresh wasabi is becoming more widely available.

won bok Chinese napa cabbage; it has white-stemmed leaves with crinkly light green tips, crunchy and mild flavored. Eaten raw, pickled or cooked.

won ton Chinese dumpling filled with meat, seafood and vegetables, served in a broth or deep-fried.

won ton mein Won ton served with noodles in a hot broth.

yokan maki Azuki beans wrapped in a cake layer.

GEOGRAPHIC INDEX

NU'UANU · KALIHI

Where to eat:

OTHER

INDEX